I0126271

Volume

1

MORTGAGE LENDING

Home Mortgage Loan Processing

Copyright © 2011 Kenney
All rights reserved.
ISBN-13: 978-1-933039-35-0

Library of Congress -in-Publication Data
March 1998

10 9 8 7 6 5 4 3 2 1

The enclosed material is designed for educational purposes only. Each State may have different certification and specific guidelines. Please refer to your State for additional and future information. The information contained herein is considered correct at the time of creation but laws and regulations are updated frequently and the reader assumes the responsibility for confirming current regulations and applicable data. The publisher and author make no warranty as to the success of the individuals using the training material contained herein. The publisher and author make no warranty as to any action taken by any individual completing this program. The reader is responsible for the appropriate use of the materials and information provided. This publication is designed to provide accurate and authoritative information concerning the subject matter. All material is sold with the understanding that neither the author nor the publisher guarantees the actions of any individual making use of the inclusions. Neither the author nor the publisher is rendering a legal opinion, accounting recommendation or other professional service. If legal advice or other expert assistance is desired, the services of a legal professional or other individual should be sought. The applicable federally released forms, disclosures and notices are generated from public domain. Copyright law does apply to all intellectual materials and all rights under said law are reserved b y the copyright owner.

Coursework is available at special quantity discounts to use as premiums and sales promotions within corporate or private training programs. To obtain information or inquire about availability please write to Director, PO Box 1, Hollidaysburg, PA 16648.

NOTICE

MORTGAGE LENDING

Home Mortgage Loan Processing

I

Introduction

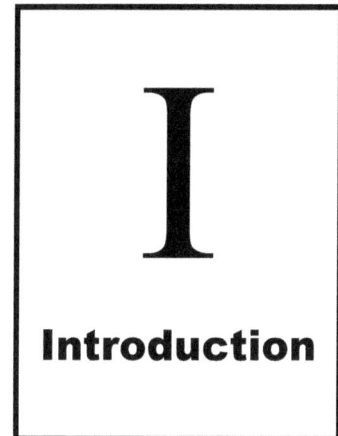

Benefits of a Mortgage Career

Congratulations on your decision to enter the mortgage-lending arena. Mortgage lending is one of the most secure, respected, and exciting career opportunities available. Each day will bring you challenges that you will overcome, the excitement of helping to create a loan program that meets the needs of both the borrower and the lender, and the satisfaction of helping each borrower achieve their dreams of homeownership. Home Mortgage Loan Processing is an excellent career opportunity that provides stability, advancement, and a sense of satisfaction to each loan processor who obtains the knowledge and skills necessary to excel within the profession.

The training contained in the course provides specific information concerning the loan process and the part you and others play in that process. The information we offer in this program provides you with the foundation that you need to become a well rounded mortgage professional. The top of your field, you will specialize in the overall picture. You will develop the perfect mix of knowledge and skills, add to it the creativity required when overcoming the specific issues that occur during the loan process, and gain the ability to reach the top of your profession.

Mortgage lending provides you with the career option that will make you one of the most highly respected professionals within your community.

As a properly trained loan processor, you will have the freedom to create your own mini-business within the security of the larger framework of the bank or brokerage for which you choose to work.

The skills you are attaining will make you a commodity that is in high-demand in the market. Loan officers need efficient loan processors to function well and to achieve success. Underwriters rely on well-trained loan processors to ensure competently prepared loan files. Lending institutions depend on carefully trained and customer service oriented loan processors to enhance their reputation as a lender who cares about the overall experience of each borrower

The room for advancement within the field of home mortgage lending is tremendous. Mortgage lending is a growing industry. This continued growth creates a constant need for properly trained professionals. You will be an integral part of this industry from the first day on the job. As an important part of the industry, you will prove your desire, drive, and abilities daily and thus ensure that advancement opportunities come your way.

Loan processing is more than just processing paper. You will be involved in nearly every aspect of the loan. Lending is an exciting industry that fulfills the dreams of your borrowers. A primary portion of your new position will be to assist every individual in overcoming any issue that arises during the loan process that may delay or even stop the loan closing. You will play an essential role in ensuring that each borrower whose file comes across your desk fulfills their dream and becomes a homeowner.

The satisfaction you receive from a job well done will keep you excited to return to work each day. Your loan officer and loan office will have small goals as well as large goals. You will be one of the most important components in reaching those goals.

➢ As a mortgage processor who conducts their business based upon a solid foundation of knowledge and core best practices, you will gain the ability to choose the environment in which you wish to work.

   You may choose to conduct your business

      From your home

      In an office

      Within a bank

➢ You will receive an income that relates directly to how hard (or smart) you work.

   The primary basis of the pay structure within the mortgage industry is the number of loans closed and the dollar value or each loan package. Dollar value includes the face amount of the loan and any interest, points and other costs incorporated into the loan package. This structure enables you to expand your income to heights that are unattainable in other, similar career options!

➤ You will build your around a core customer base of satisfied borrowers.

Each time you create the perfect loan package for a borrower, oversee a perfect loan process, and ensure a smooth closing meeting, you grow your business. The borrowers you work with today will be the referral sources upon which you will build your business. Regardless of where you go within the industry, your exceptional customer service will ensure that your borrowers will go with you.

➤ You will obtain the freedom available only through being the in charge of your career.

A loan processor is one of the few individuals who have the ability to blend the respect of being an independent business professional with the security of working under the umbrella of a corporate environment and the flexibility of being in charge of their own business!

➤ You will have the opportunity to use your creativity and ingenuity to become the best in your chosen profession.

Loan stipulations are in place for each lending source that you will work with during your career. The ability to assist the borrower in meeting these stipulations will ensure that the process flows smoothly.

Each borrower will have specific issues and situations within their lives that you must overcome during the documentation processes.

Through the application of creative thinking and a comprehensive understanding of the lending arena, you can blend the lender stipulations with the borrower situation to create the perfect loan package for every application!

Research has shown that the most important attribute of a successful loan processor is the drive to succeed. The drive to succeed surpasses educational degrees, experience and personal attributes within the field of mortgage lending. Purchasing this program shows that you have initial drive needed to begin on the path toward career stability and success and attain top-producer status.

This program will assist you in gaining the base foundation you need to begin building your new career.

Mortgage Lending is perhaps one of the most satisfying career options available. You will perform the service of allowing people to fulfill their dreams of homeownership. The industry is fast-paced, exciting and offers a stable career opportunity to anyone willing to put forth the effort to succeed. Each file you receive will contain a myriad of variations that will ensure every workday provides you with the challenge to perform at your best.

The coursework builds the foundation you will need in the coming days, months, and years. Each segment of the program builds upon the previous to ensure you gain the knowledge base that will allow you to enter your new professional with confidence and competence. The program format allows you to gain each component essential to your success in an organized and efficient manner. Each section contains a self-test whose correct completion. Upon successful completion of the coursework and an understanding of each review section, you will find that you are have a higher industry skill level then 90% of your competing loan processors.

Chapter 1

THE LENDING PROCESS

Gaining a comprehensive understanding of the lending arena and the processes that occur between the application by a borrower and the purchase of packaged closed loans on the secondary market is the first step you must take on the path to career success.

The mortgage market is divided into two classifications.

- The primary mortgage market

- The secondary mortgage market

The primary mortgage market is the area where lenders work directly with borrowers to originate, document and close loans. Examples of entities within the primary mortgage market are

- Mortgage Brokerage Office
- Savings Banks
- Commercial Banks
- Mutual Savings Bank
- Credit Union

These lending institutions work directly with borrowers who need funding to purchase real estate.

The employees who work within the mortgage department at these locations are loan processors, loan originators, mortgage brokers, and loan officers.

COMMON TITLES

A **Loan Originator** is someone who spends a great part of the workday on the streets soliciting borrower referrals from affinity groups. They bring these borrower referrals back to their office, structure the loan package that meets the borrowers needs, and document a package that will enable the lending institution to fund a solid loan. The act of being an originator means that your primary focus is to originate loans.

A **Loan Officer** is someone who spends a great deal of his or her time in the office, interviewing potential borrowers and structuring the available loan products to meet the needs and specific situation of the borrower. The primary goal of the loan officer is to ensure that each loan closed provides all of the parties involved with the best possible loan package.

A **Mortgage Broker** is someone who uses their vast knowledge of the mortgage industry to bring potential borrower packages to the right lending institution and obtain the loan program that meets the needs of both the borrower and lender. The broker acts as a liaison bringing the potential borrowers together with the right lender and loan program to ensure that the borrower achieves their dreams of homeownership.

A **Loan Processor** assists the borrower in obtaining all of the documents and services that are required to complete the loan process and purchase transaction. The essential element of the loan-processing career is to act as a liaison between the borrower and all other individuals whose assistance is required to achieve a closed loan. The loan processor's primary focus during the loan process is to complete all of the necessary tasks in a timely manner and that all items incorporated into the closing package are correct and free of errors.

Each of these individuals will work directly with the borrower to accomplish the tasks that lead to a home loan funding.

- Complete the mortgage loan application or 1003.

- Obtain loan stipulations or documentation required by the stipulations list or sales agreement.

- Order affiliate services such as Title Searches and Appraisals.

- Generate the borrower's good faith estimate.

- Provide all required disclosures and notifications to the borrower.

- Structure the mortgage loan funding and borrower down payment to meet the parameters of the loan approval.

- Arrange and oversee the borrowers closing on the property.

Many borrowers assume that the bank where they make the loan application funds the mortgage loans through available cash resulting from the deposits of the individuals who conduct their banking activity at that bank. In some cases, this is exactly where the funds required to provide a mortgage loan originate. However, these depository funds are often inadequate to meet the borrowing needs of all of the individuals who obtain loan proceeds from the local institution.

SECONDARY MORTGAGE MARKET

Lenders within the primary mortgage market will underwrite and fund mortgage loans that the borrower applies for with the cash that they have on hand. Once the lender has a group of funded loan packages, they will combine the many funded loan packages into one large package and offer it for sale to the secondary mortgage market.

The secondary mortgage market includes entities such as

- Insurance Companies
- Primary Lenders with excess deposits
- Pension Funds
- Individual Investors

The secondary mortgage market purchases funded and closed loans from the direct lender in the primary mortgage market.

- This purchase of the closed loans enables the banks and institutions within the primary market to fund more loans than would be possible if they had to fund and service all of the debt load within their portfolio themselves.

- This funding enables the entities on the secondary market to obtain the return on their investment generated through the interest and penalty figures applied to the borrowed funds.

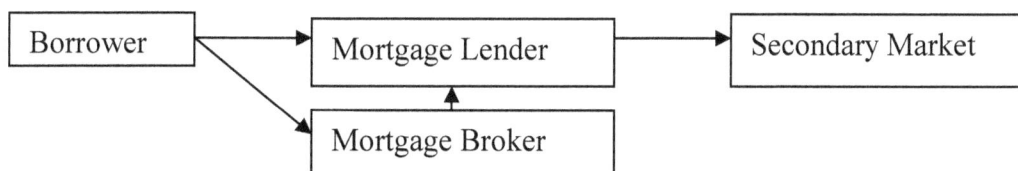

Figure 1:1 Mortgage Market Structure

1. The borrower makes a mortgage application with mortgage loan officer or mortgage loan processor who works in a Mortgage Bank that funds its own loans or in a Mortgage Brokerage that works with multiple funding sources.

2. The mortgage lender provides the borrower with the funds to purchase the home.

3. The mortgage bank or loan funding institution completes this process as many times as possible with the funds that they have available.

4. The mortgage bank or loan funding institution then packages the loan with other loans that have been funded with their capital.

    ▪ If the overall loan package is large enough (worth enough money), the funding institution offers that package for sale to investors within the secondary mortgage market.

    ▪ If the mortgage-funding source does not have enough loan products to package into large enough groups to meet the needs of the secondary mortgage market, they will package them into a smaller grouping and offer the package to another lending institution or a smaller investing group.

      This smaller group of investors forms what is termed an investing pool. An investing pool can include anyone who is seeking a low risk, long-term investment and has the capital available to purchase the packaged loan products.

      This investing pool will then collect the interest on the loans that they have purchased and achieve the return on their capital investment that meets their needs.

    ▪ If the loans are packaged and sold to another lending institution, that institution will package the purchased loans with their own funded loan packages and create an overall offering large enough for the secondary mortgage market.

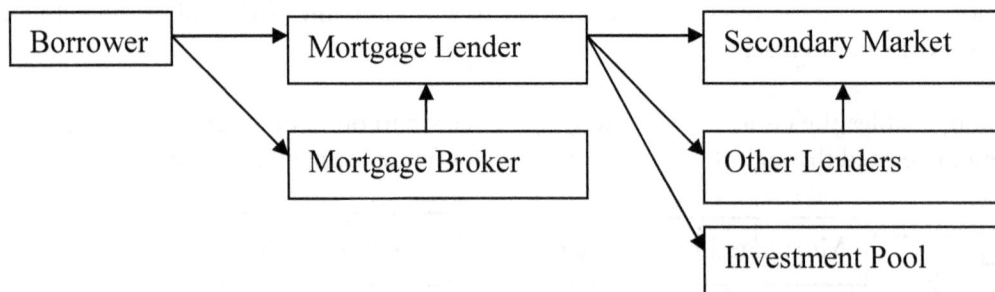

Figure 1:2 Expanded Mortgage Market Structure

As a loan processor, you will play a critical part in the success of all of these entities. The fundamental beginning that enables all of the described processes to function will rest on the work you will complete in assisting borrowers in fulfilling all of the stipulations required to obtain loan approval and close the loan package. You will complete these tasks for either a mortgage bank or a mortgage brokerage.

BANKING VS BROKERING

The first decision you will make as a loan processor is whether you will choose to create your business within the structure of a traditional banking institution or within a mortgage brokerage. Included within this decision is whether you will base your office out of a home office or within the conventional environment of the mortgage bank or brokerage.

Working in a Bank

A bank is a lending institution that typically underwrites, processes, and funds mortgage loans with their own money. The benefits of working with a traditional banking environment are obvious.

- Traditional banking institutions are typically located within the community that they serve. Working within a recognized community institution will provide you with name recognition that gives your borrowers an immediate sense of reliability.

- Traditional lenders often retain their own team of loan underwriters, processors, closers, and post-closers that will enable you to create a "team" atmosphere that may assist in smoother loan processes and closings.

- The loans that you originate and process will be funded by the bank for which you work. This in-house funding typically creates a smoother loan process in that the underwriters will usually not change the loan terms, stipulations, or requirements after you have obtained an initial approval of the application.

Working for a bank also has its downside.

- A bank will have a limited number of products available and these will have very specific guidelines.

  The limited program availability from a bank means, if your borrower does not fit within those guidelines, they will be declined.

  Since you will only have access to the products or loan types offered by the bank for which you work, a borrower who is declined for your loan products will need to "shop" other lenders to obtain their mortgage loan.

- Banks are more likely to have only "A" paper product available. This limited product availability limits your borrowers to those who have "A" credit. Most banks do have additional programs for those B/C borrowers who fall just below the A Paper criteria but the programs are typically not as competitive as the products your Brokering competition can locate.

This lack of product availability will place limitations on how large your personal business is able to grow because you will only be able to work with those borrowers in your region who meet the specified guidelines of your bank. The remaining borrowers will work with another loan processor.

Working in a Brokerage

A Mortgage Broker acts as a liaison between the borrower seeking mortgage funds and multiple funding sources. The mortgage brokerage will typically not fund any loans but will fulfills the task of shopping for the perfect loan to meet each borrowers specific situation and mortgage needs.

- A Broker typically works with multiple lenders enabling them to offer a variety of loan programs. You will find most Brokerages have contracted to write loans for between 40 and 200 different lenders. This variety allows you to shop many programs making it relatively easy to find an approval program for more of the loan applications that you originate.

- As a loan processor with a mortgage brokerage, you will have the ability to obtain competing approvals for the funding of each loan application that you process. Rather than one cut and dried approval that may kill your deal at the time of loan application, you should be able to find options that allow you to customize the loan program to suit your borrower's needs.

   Example: Lender 1 approves the borrower's application with a low interest rate but requires that the borrower place a large amount of money down as a contingency of the approval.

           Issue: Your borrowers are cash poor but are willing to make a higher monthly payment.

           Solution: You locate another lender within your contracts that is willing to fund the loan at a slightly higher interest rate in exchange for the borrower's ability to place less money down.

Working at a mortgage brokerage also has some inherent disadvantages that you would need to overcome.

- You are not on the same "team" as your underwriters, closers and post-closers but you will find that if you build respectful rapport with these individuals your goals are the same – closed loans.

- Mortgage Brokerage offices are typically not as recognizable within the community. Banking institutions offer many services to their customers beyond the mortgage loan service enabling the loan officer within the bank to originate more borrowers from the customer base of the bank. A mortgage brokerage typically offers only loan services. This will limit the name recognition of the company within the community and the available customer pool will be related only to the mortgage processes rather than a diverse group of customer offerings.

Regardless of the employment method you choose, there are as many ways to put a loan package together as there are borrowers in your town. It will be up to you to combine your knowledge of the industry and the products available to you with the essential drive and creativity that led you to the lending arena.

Working from Home

Many banks and brokerages are now hiring loan processors as full W-2 employees and enabling them to base their business out of their own home. These loan processors process and document loan packages in the same manner as the more conventional specialists working out of an office.

Some banks and brokerages will hire a loan processor who will e-commute and blend the two location options to customize their business around their lifestyle. A loan processor working in this manner will spend a portion of their time in the office and the remainder of their time working from home.

- Through e-commuting or setting your office up entirely out of your home, you will be able to customize your career around your lifestyle and family to create the career option that will enable you to excel within the industry.

- You will be able to use the resources of the bank or brokerage for which you work during your in-office time but service your customers from your home office enabling you to build a customer base that depends entirely on you. If you transfer positions or companies, you will retain the customer base you have built providing you with a solid foundation upon which to build your career.

- You will be an employee with all of the benefits of W-2 employment while you retain the freedom and independence of being your own boss.

There are varieties of positions available within the Mortgage Lending arena to suit your personal goals, needs and personalized career path. You will customize your career path around your situation, desired level of managerial input, and the freedom you need to build your career successfully.

Upon completion of this coursework, you will be better trained than 90% of the loan processors currently employed within the mortgage industry. You will be an asset in the industry with the ability to build your career to suit your needs and desired level of success.
We will review materials concerning charting your career and negotiating a position in the Career Tools segment. Throughout your training you should continue to consider what environment would most benefit you and we will provide the foundation of knowledge, industry skills, and tools you need to achieve success in that environment.

Chapter 2

ETHICS AND DISCLOSURES

The Federal Government and most State Governments have established laws and acts that you will use to create the policies and procedures with which you handle each potential borrower and business contact.

These laws are in place to protect the interest of the public and to make the obtainment of housing and home mortgage funds a fair practice for all applicants. You must incorporate the required practices into your daily task list to ensure you disclose all of the required information to your borrowers.

Another facet of your job is borrower education. As a professionally trained home-mortgage loan processor, you must act in an ethically sound way and educate the borrower to assist them in gaining the knowledge that they need to protect themselves in the future.

Many States are in the process of or have completed the implementation of required licensure training for home-mortgage loan processors. One goal of this educational training is to ensure that you have the necessary knowledge base to protect your borrowers, inform the consumers, and behave in an ethical manner that complies with all federal and state statues and laws.

During this section, we will address specific guidelines of behavior and disclosure that are in place and strive to make you as well educated concerning these laws as possible.

Learning the materials included will assist not only your borrower but also your overall career success. Adherence to the guidelines and laws we will review will prove your dedication to professionalism and raise your customer service beyond that of much of your competition.

You are entering a professional career much like that of a physician or attorney and you must ensure that your behavior and actions are above reproach.

Home Mortgage Disclosure Act

The Home Mortgage Disclosure Act (H. M. D. A.) was enacted by Congress in 1975 and implemented by the Federal Reserve Boards Regulation C. This act requires lending institutions to report public loan data.

This data is used to aid in determining whether financial institutions are serving the housing needs of their communities. Public officials use this data to determine the need for the distribution of public-sector investments and to attract private investment to areas where it is will be of use. The data also helps to identify possible discriminatory lending patterns.

This regulation applies to certain financial institutions, including banks, savings associations, credit unions, and other mortgage lending institutions. Using the loan data submitted by these financial institutions, the Federal Financial Institutions Examination Council creates aggregate and disclosure reports for each metropolitan area.

You should gather the information for the report at the time the 1008 and 1003 are completed. Much of the information required for reports a part of the standard 1003 application. The obtainment of this data should be a regulated portion of your application interview. Obtaining the correct data at the time of application ensures that you maintain concise reporting activity.

The H. M. D. A. REPORT will contain identifying details relating to the specific loan package.

SAMPLE HMDA REPORT

Applicant(s) Name_____
Loan Officer Name: _____ Lender Name: _____
Property Address: _____
Date of Application: _____

LOAN TYPE:
__1. Conventional
__2. FHA
__3. VA
__4. Other

PROPERTY TYPE:
__1. Single Family
__2. Manufactured Housing
__3. Multifamily

LOAN PURPOSE:
__1. Home Purchase
__2. Home Improvement
__3. Cash-out Refinance
__4. Rate/Term Refinance

OCCUPANCY:
__1. Owner Occupied
__2. Non-Owner Occupied

ACTION TAKEN:
__1. Loan originated
__2. Application approved but not accepted
__3. Application denied
__4. Counter-offer denied
__5. Application withdrawn by applicant

APPLICATION TYPE:
__1. By Mail
__2. By Phone
__3. Face-to-Face
__4. Internet

REASONS FOR DENIAL:
    __1. Excessive Debt to income ratio
    __2. Insufficient Employment history
    __3. Credit history
    __4. Collateral
    __5. Insufficient cash available
    __6. Other _____

2:1 Sample Form – HMDA – HUD Release Continued

HMDA REPORT EXPLANATION

Date of Application

The date your office receives the application or the date shown on the application form will be the date you use for reporting. The basis of the reporting and disclosure action timelines is the date on the form.

Loan Type

Indicates whether the loan granted, applied for, or purchased was non-conventional, conventional, government-guaranteed, or government-insured.

If the loan falls in an unconventional or special category, you will select the option "Other" and enter a descriptive heading for the type of loan.

Property Type

The specific type of property must be on the report. The choices for property type are

Single Family
Manufactured Housing
Multifamily

Loan Purpose

Each applicant will be making the loan application for a specific purpose. The planned use of the loan funds affects the handling of the loan process. You will include the purpose details with in the report.

Home Purchase
Home Improvement
Cash-out Refinance.
Rate and Term Refinance

You should select multifamily dwelling regardless of the loan type for dwellings that are five-or-more families.

Occupancy

The type of occupancy relating to the property will also dictate many of the application, processing, and funding related actions. The property will be either

Owner Occupied
Non-Owner Occupied

Action Taken Type The action taken type field defines the disposition of the loan application.

Loan originated
Application approved but not accepted
Application denied
Counter-offer denied
Application withdrawn by applicant

Action Taken Date If the application results in a closed loan, you will enter the settlement or closing date of the loan.

If the application does not result in an origination, you will enter the date of the cancellation request or the date when your office sent the notice of denial to the applicant.

If the applicant expressly withdrew the application, you will enter either the date shown on the applicant's withdrawal letter, or the date you received the letter or notice.

For loans that an institution purchased, you will enter the date of the purchase.

Application Type The type of application or method of making the application dictates the timelines for the remittal of certain disclosures. You will define the method that the borrower used to make the loan application within the report.

By Mail
By Phone
Face-to-Face
Over the Internet

Reasons For Denial If the loan application results in a denial from underwriting, you must define the reasons for the denial. Common reasons for an application denial are on the report and include

Excessive debt to income ratio
Insufficient employment history
Credit history
Collateral

Insufficient cash available

If the denial of the application pertains to another factor of the file, you will enter a description of that reason in the area labeled other.

Applicant Race

The government will monitor the handling of files as they relate to each segment of society. This monitoring helps to ensure that all individuals have access to fair lending opportunities. One monitoring segment relates to the race or national origin of the applicant.

This reporting encompasses originated loans and loan applications that do not result in an origination.

Applicant Sex

A secondary monitoring classification is the gender of the applicant

This reporting applies for originated loans and for loan applications that do not result in an origination

Census Tract/BNA

A Census Tract identifies a statistical subdivision of a county.

Census Tract numbers ranges from 0001.00 to 9499.99. The number assigned to an area is unique within a county.

A Block Numbering Area (BNA) identifies a subdivision of a county. The purpose of the BNA is to enable the grouping and numbering blocks in non-metropolitan counties where local census committees have not established census tracts.

BNA numbers range from 9501.00 to 9989.99 and are unique within a county.

Census Tracts and BNAs are mutually exclusive. Thus, these statistical areas do not overlap. There is a census tract or BNA number for every area of the United States.

County Code

Each geographical area receives a three-digit Federal Information Processing Standards code. This code identifies the county where the property is located.

Dwelling

Dwelling means any residential structure whether or not it is attached to real property. The term dwelling includes condominiums, cooperative units and mobile or manufactured homes.

It refers to single family and multifamily structures.

16

Recreational vehicles such as boats or campers are not dwellings under HMDA.

Loan Application Number   Each loan will be assigned a unique identifier of up to 25 characters.

It is recommended that institutions do not use applicant's names or social security numbers as part of the loan application number. This helps to ensure the privacy of the borrower.

Fair Housing

Fair housing laws are in place to prevent discrimination against any borrower in the sale, rental, financing, or other housing related transaction. The law prohibits the discrimination against any borrower based upon race, color, national origin, religion, sex, familial status, and handicap. A recent executive order also states that practices must eliminate, to the extent possible, barriers arising from a limited proficiency in English in the use or participation in any federally conducted program.

The Federal Fair Housing Act prohibits the use of discriminatory advertising that state a preference for a particular type of person. You may not advertise in a manner meant to attract or deter a potential borrower based on race, color, religion, sex, handicap, familial status, or national origin. HUD released a clarification of acceptable words and phrases that you can use when generating advertisements. You must use caution when composing your advertising so as not to include any item that is discriminatory in nature. More information regarding acceptable advertising is included in the Advanced Mortgage Marketing Course or you can obtain details relating to appropriate advertising practices directly from HUD.

The nature of advertising allows you a broad spectrum in which to operate. It is important to remember that discrimination in real estate practice is illegal. Providing you are not targeting particular strata of society for either positive or negative effect, staying within the guidelines is relatively easy.

Federal Agencies evaluate their policies and programs on a regular basis to determine any modifications that must be made relating to a protected class under the fair housing laws.

Along with the Fair Housing Act, the Equal Credit Opportunity Acts establishes guidelines and regulations regarding potential discrimination against borrowers. The following sections further describe practices that should and should not be employed in relationship to your borrowers. Following the explanatory sections are sample disclosures you must provide to each applicant.

Equal Credit Opportunity Act/Fair Housing Act

The Equal Credit Opportunity and the Fair Housing Acts ensure that all consumers are given the same opportunity to obtain credit.

What this does not mean is that an applicant who does not meet guidelines will obtain credit.

What this does mean is that all credit applicants must receive a level consideration regardless of outside factors or personal considerations.

Pre-qualification services must be provided to all borrowers equally. It is illegal to include discriminatory factors as criteria for the determination on a loan package.

The Equal Credit Opportunity Act and Fair Housing Act identify a number of factors that are illegal to use in evaluating an applicants qualifications.

> Race, Color, Religion, Sex, National Origin, Marital Status, Age (provided the applicant is capable of entering a legally binding contract), Source of Income, Handicap and Familial Status

A lender may decline an oral or written application as long as the decline is based upon legitimate underwriting standards applied to all loan packages and not based upon one of the prohibited items.

A loan processor must understand the difference between an "inquiry" and an "application". Many requirements apply only to applications. The regulations describe a loan application as *"An oral or written request for an extension of credit that is made in accordance with the procedures established by a creditor for the credit type listed"*.

Procedures established refer to the actual practices followed by a creditor for making credit decisions as well as its stated application procedures.

It is important to establish your particular employer's standards as they relate to the application or inquiry distinction. The quick list of required disclosures included in the appendix segment of your workbook combines the disclosure requirements at application into one checklist chart. You should refer often to this chart to ensure you are providing the required documents to all borrowers at the correct time and in the correct manner.

The Equal Credit Opportunity Act protects against other items beyond credit discrimination. It has provisions in place regarding predatory lending tactics and abusive activities with in the lending arena.

Creditors must provide applicants with notices of the actions taken on their credit application. These notices include approvals, counteroffers, and credit denial.

- Approval notices provide the applicant with specific information regarding the loan program for which they have been approved.

- A counteroffer is an approval notice that contains different terms than those that the applicant originally requested. A counteroffer notice provides vital information to the applicant in the event the loan terms are changed between the date of application and the date of closing.

KENNEY

Changes between the application and closing can occur for a variety of reasons.

Example: A borrower makes application with one property in mind.

The offer for that property is not accepted.

The borrower chooses a different property with slightly different contract terms.

Action: You will alter the loan offering to conform to the new property contract.

Changes to the loan between application and closing may also occur for less respectable reasons.

Example: A lender may alter the terms of the loan to incorporate additional fees into the principal borrowed.

Example: A lender offering a second mortgage may alter the terms of the loan to incorporate a refinance of the first mortgage and therefore improve their lien position and increase the loan amount funded.

These tactics, among others, fall within the term predatory lending. These tactics are unlawful under federal lending acts.

The full disclosure of any action taken on a credit application will ensure that your practices remain impeccable.

FINANCIAL DISCRIMINATION ACT
FAIR LENIDNG NOTICE

It is illegal to discriminate based on

1. Trends, characteristics, or conditions in a neighborhood unless the financial institution is able to demonstrate that such consideration is required to ensure safety

2. Race, color, religion, sex, marital status, familial status, national origin, ancestry, or handicap

It is illegal to consider the racial, ethnic, religious, or national origin composition of a neighborhood or geographic area surrounding a housing accommodation or whether such composition is undergoing change.

These provisions govern financial assistance for the purpose of purchase, construction, rehabilitation, or refinancing of one to four unit residences occupied by the owner.

If you have any questions about your rights, or if you wish to file a complaint you may contact:

2:2 Sample Form – Financial Discrimination Act Fair Lending Notice – HUD Release

Federal Equal Credit Opportunity Act Notice

The Federal Equal Credit Opportunity Act prohibits creditors from discriminating against credit applicants on the basis of color, religion, national origin, sex, marital status, age (provided the applicant has the capacity to enter into a binding contract), because all of part of the applicant's income is derived from public assistance programs, or because the applicant has in good faith exercised any right under the Consumer Protection Act

Lending institutions are prohibited from bringing up certain specific subjects that lend themselves to discrimination. These subjects are as follows:

> Whether or not an applicant has or will have children.

> Whether or not there exist childcare problems.

> Whether or not there will be interruptions of income due to childbirth.

> Whether or not an applicant is receiving alimony, child support, or separate maintenance unless this income is voluntarily disclosed as a source of additional income to be considered as part of the credit application

> Whether an applicant is widowed, divorced, or single

> Whether or not an applicant's telephone number is publicly listed

Lending institutions must take and report actions taken on your applications within a reasonable time. If the application is denied, the reason for the denial must be provided if requested.

I/we acknowledge that we received a copy of this notice:

2:3 Sample Form – Federal Equal Credit Opportunity Act Notice – HUD Release

Credit Information Disclosure Authorization

I / We _____ Borrower Name _____ , _____ Co-Borrower Name _____ hereby authorize you to release to Mortgage Company Name information for verification purposes.

This information may include:

> Employment information including past and present employers

> Banking and Savings Account Records

> Mortgage Loan Rating Information

> Rental History Information

> A consumer credit report from a credit-reporting agency

This information is for the confidential use in processing an application for a real estate loan

A copy of this authorization and applicable signature(s) may be deemed the equivalent of the original.

2:4 Sample Form – Credit Information Disclosure Authorization – HUD Release

KENNEY

Whenever information is gathered about an individual including credit reports, employment history, financial institution data, and tax return information, a release for such information gathering must be completed by the borrower.

During the transaction, the loan processor, loan officer, underwriter, or other individuals involved in completing the loan process will obtain information from multiple sources that enable them to assess the creditworthiness of the borrower and their ability to repay the debt.

All borrowers must sign a credit and information release authorization before you begin the process of collecting the applicable data. You will incorporate a copy of this authorization into any documentation request that you make during the loan process. It is critical that you ensure you obtain the applicable signatures on this form since obtaining credit data, including the credit report, without the applicable authorization violates the rights of the borrower.

CREDIT BUREAU NOTICE TO THE HOME APPLICANT

Trans Union Corporation (Empirica)

_____
Current Score   Date of Score

_____
Range of Score

Key Factors:

Equifax Information Services (Beacon)

_____
Current Score   Date of Score

_____
Range of Score

Key Factors:

Exprian Information Services (Fair Isaac)

_____
Current Score   Date of Score

_____
Range of Score

Key Factors:

In connection with your application for a home loan, we must disclose to you the score that a credit bureau distributed to users and in connection with your home loan and the key factors affecting your credit score.

The credit score is a computer-generated summary calculated at the time of the request and based on information a credit bureau or lender has on file. The scores are based on data about your credit history and payment patterns. Credit scores are important because they are used to assist the lender in determining whether you will obtain a loan. They may also be used to determine what interest rate may be offered on the mortgage. Credit scores can change over time, depending on your conduct, how your credit history and payment patterns change, and how credit-scoring technologies change.

Because the score is based on information in your credit history, it is very important that you review the credit-related information that is being furnished to make sure it is accurate. Credit records may vary from one company to another.

If you have questions about your credit score or the credit information that is furnished to you, contact the credit bureau at the address and telephone number provided.

The credit bureau plays no part in the decision to take action on the loan application and is unable to provide you with specific reasons for the decision on a loan application.

2:5 Sample Form – Credit Bureau Notice to the Home Applicant – HUD Release

In addition to the credit release authorization, you must provide the borrower with information indicating how their credit worthiness was determined. This disclosure notice explains

- The scores received from the bureaus.

- The factors contributing to the scores

- The fact that the bureaus do not make a credit determination but rather report the inclusions of the credit profile

Contact information and directions to inquire into the credit profile will often be incorporated into the disclosure.

Real Estate Settlement Procedures Act (RESPA)

The Real Estate Settlement Procedures Act is enforced by HUD and deals with closing costs and settlement procedures. The purpose of the act is to regulate the processes of closing practices across the United States. The Real Estate Settlement Procedures Act prohibits specific practices in relationship to the transfer of property involving a first mortgage loan on a one to four unit dwellings.

The purposes of RESPA are to:

- Help consumers in shopping for settlement services.

- Eliminate referral fees that increase the costs of certain settlement services.

The act requires that borrowers receive disclosures at various times during the mortgage application and home purchase processes.

The act prohibits a person from giving or accepting any thing of value for referrals of settlement service business.

The act prohibits a person from giving or accepting any part of a charge for services that are not performed.

The act prohibits home sellers from requiring homebuyers to purchase title insurance from a particular company.

The act restricts the amount of property tax and insurance payments that may be paid in advance at or prior to the closing of a home loan.

> The amount of property tax or insurance payments that may be paid in advance by a borrower is limited to the owner's share of the taxes and insurance that is due at the time of settlement

plus $1/6^{th}$ of the amount that will become due for these items within the 12-month period following settlement.

The Federal Government as well as most State Governing bodies has established laws and acts that you will use to create the policies and procedures with which you handle each potential closing and business contact.

These laws are in place to protect the interest of the public and to make the obtainment of housing and home mortgage funds a fair practice for all applicants. You must incorporate the required practices into your daily task list to ensure that you handle each closing task in compliance with the requirements.

You are entering a professional career much like that of a physician or attorney and you must ensure that your behavior and actions are above reproach.

Required Disclosures at Application

At the time of application, mortgage brokers or lenders must give the borrowers

- An Information Booklet containing consumer information regarding various real estate settlement services.

- A Good Faith Estimate of settlement costs. This lists the charges the buyer is likely to pay at settlement. This is only an estimate and the actual charges may differ.

- If a lender requires the borrower to use a particular settlement provider, then the lender must disclose this requirement on the good faith estimate.

- A Mortgage Servicing Disclosure Statement that defines for the borrower whether the lender intends to service the loan or transfer it to another lender.

The lender gives these disclosures to the borrower at the time of a face-to-face application or mails it to them within three business days of receiving a mail, internet, or telephone loan application.

If the lender turns down the loan within three days, then the Real Estate Settlement Procedures Act does not require the lender to provide these documents.

When is an Application an Application?

ECOA and RESPA disclosures must be provided the borrower within a specified amount of time following an application. This brings up the question of when an application is an application. The date determination for the completion of an application will vary depending on the method used by the borrower when making the application.

> At the time of a face-to-face interview, customers must sign the 1003 application. The date and time of this signature is considered the date of the application.

  You will check face-to-face interview in the box labeled "to be completed by interviewer" on page 3 of the 1003.

> The application is considered complete at the time the branch or loan processor receives the application by mail, special delivery, or through another remote means.

  You will check "by mail" in the box labeled "to be completed by interviewer" on page 3 of the 1003.

  You will enter the date the application was received in the office.

> If the information was obtained over the telephone, and you enter the data into the 1003 on behalf of the borrower, you will Check "by telephone" in the box labeled "to be completed by interviewer" on page 3 of the 1003.

  You will then send the completed 1003 to the applicant for signature.

  You should send copies of the GFE, TIL, and HUD Guide and Compliance books along with the blank application form. The date of the application will be the date the completed 1003 and signed disclosures are received in the office.

  *   It should be noted that if a potential borrower wishes to apply "by mail" they must be sent a BLANK 1003 application.

      Mail applications would normally be in the applicants own handwriting.

  *   Loan applications completed by an individual from your office are never considered a mail application. Information taken from a customer over the telephone would constitute a "telephone application".

HMDA forms are completed, in part, from Section X of the 1003 labeled "Information for Government Monitoring Purposes". This data must be completed for all applications even if the application is not a face-to-face interview.

Applicants do not have to provide answers to these questions. If an applicant does not wish to provide government-monitoring information, they should check "I do not wish to provide this information" on the application.

The completion date of the 1003 will set the time for the remittal of other disclosures.

➤ The Good Faith Estimate and the Truth-In-Lending Statement should be provided to the borrower at the time of face-to-face meeting if the application is a face-to-face application.

  If the application is completed by mail, the good faith estimate and truth in lending statement should be sent within three business days of receipt of the mail application.

  If the application is a telephone application, the good faith estimate and truth in lending statement should be sent within three business days of the completion of the telephone application.

➤ The charm or Consumer Handbook on Adjustable Rate Mortgages must be provided to all ARM applicants at the time of face-to-face interview, must be mailed to all ARM applicants within three business days of receipt of mail application or completion of the telephone interview.

➤ The Affiliated Business Arrangement notice, the Appraisal Notice, the Servicing Disclosure, the rate float or lock option form, and a copy of the HUD Guide and Compliance booklet must be given to the applicant at time of a face-to-face interview or mailed within three business days of the date of receipt of a mail application or completion of a telephone application.

Applicants must sign and date an Acknowledgement illustrating the receipt of these disclosures. You should retain a copy of each acknowledged disclosure in the loan file.

If the application is a mail or telephone application, you should mail a copy of all of the applicable disclosures to the applicant with either a blank application or a copy of the telephone completed application. You should include a letter instructing the applicant to return a signed and dated copy of each Acknowledgement document.

Disclosures

	face-to-face	Mail	Telephone
ECOA: When is an ap an ap?	At the time of face-to-face interview when the 1003 is completed Customers must sign the 1003 application. Check face-to-face interview in the box labeled "to be completed by interviewer" on page 3 of the 1003.	At the time, the branch or loan officer received the application. Check "by mail" in the box labeled "to be completed by interviewer" on page 3 of the 1003. Enter the date the application was received.	At the time, information for the 1003 was obtained over the telephone. Check "by telephone" in the box labeled "to be completed by interviewer" on page 3 of the 1003. Send the 1003 to the applicant for signature, along with copies of the GFE, TIL, and HUD Guide/ Compliance booklets.
		NOTE: Customers wanting to apply "by mail" must be sent a BLANK 1003 application. Mail applications would therefore normally be in the applicant's own handwriting.	Loan applications completed by the Loan Officers are never considered a mail application. Information taken from a customer over the telephone would constitute a "telephone application".
HMDA: Section X "Information for Government Monitoring Purposes"	Must be completed for all applications even an applicant is not present at the time the application is completed. Applicants do not have to provide information: they should check "I do not wish to provide this information" in the applicable section of the 1003. The Loan Officer may make a "best guess" regarding this information based on visual observation or surname. The LO should note on page 3 that information was "BVO" (based on visual observation).	Section X does not have to be completed by the applicant when they complete a mail application. It is not necessary to ask applicants for this information if the application is returned to the office with these areas blank. The Loan Officer will mark "I do not wish to provide this information" on the 1003 if the applicant did not do so. No further information is necessary.	Section X does not have to be completed by the applicant when they complete a telephone application. If the applicant does not wish to provide this information, the Loan Officer will mark "I do not wish to provide this information" on the 1003. No further information is necessary.
RESPA/TIL: Good Faith Estimate (GFE) & Truth-In-Lending Statement (TIL)	At the time of face-to-face meeting or sent within three business days of application date if prepared by the branch.	Mail within three business days of receipt of their mail application	Mail within three business days of the completion of a telephone application
CHARM: Consumer Handbook on Adjustable Rate Mortgage	Must be provided to all ARM applicants at the time of face-to-face interview	Must be mailed to all ARM applicants within three business days of receipt of mail application	Must be mailed to all ARM applicants within three business days of the completion of a telephone application
RESPA Affiliated Business Arrangement ECOA Appraisal Notice RESPA Servicing Disclosure FLOAT/LOCK FORM	Provide copy to applicants at the time of the face-to-face appearance. Applicants must sign and date an Acknowledgement illustrating that they received the applicable disclosures. You should retain copy in the loan file.	Mail to applicants with the blank application. You should include instructions to the applicant to return the signed and dated Acknowledgement documents. Retain copy of the signed and dated Acknowledgement in loan file.	Mail to applicants along with the completed 1003, GFE, and TIL. You should include instructions to the applicant to return the signed and dated Acknowledgement documents. Retain copy of the signed and dated Acknowledgement in loan file.

2:6 Disclosure Reference Chart

THE GOOD FAITH ESTIMATE

It is essential that you understand the components of a Good Faith Estimate and gain the knowledge necessary to generate the estimate. The inclusions on the good faith estimate serve many functions during the loan process from assisting in the creation of the HUD 1 Settlement Statement to setting borrower expectations with regard to the costs that they will incur during the obtainment of their mortgage loan. Setting the expectations of costs at the proper level is one of the most important acts that you can perform. This single act is essential to ensuring smooth closings and good relationships – with your borrowers, with the real estate offices, with the closing agents, and with your closing team!

Many of the costs involved in closing a loan including appraisal fees, pest inspections, and title costs are standard in the industry or in the region where you conduct your business.

Your funding source will require you to charge other costs that are specific to the funding source and may vary among different lenders. You will want to refer to your underwriting guidelines to determine what fees a particular lender requires.

Other costs in the good faith estimate are part of your offices payment structure. These costs should remain similar for all borrowers. It is inappropriate to charge one borrower a $500.00 application fee and another borrower a $50.00 application fee.

In general, the structure and inclusions of the good faith estimate will depend on the type of loan you are processing, the funding source of the loan, and the transaction details negotiated within the sales agreement and dictated by the lending approval.

Mortgage Lending – Home Mortgage Loan Processing

Lender:
Address:

Applicant(s):

Property Address:

Sales Price:
    Base Loan Amount:
Total Loan Amount:
Interest Rate:
Type of Loan:

Preparation Date:
Loan Number

The information provided below reflects estimates of the charges which you are likely to incur at the settlement of your loan. The fees   listed are estimates – actual charges may be more or less. Your transaction may not involve a fee for every item listed. THE NUMBERS LISTED BESIDE THE ESTIMATES GENERALLY CORRESPOND TO THE NUMBERED LINES CONTAINED THE HUD-1 OR HUD-1A SETTLEMENT STATEMENT WHICH YOU WILL BE RECEIVEING AT THE SETTLEMENT. THE HUD-1 OR HUD-1A SETTLEMENT STATEMENT WILL SHOW YOU THE ACTUAL COST FOR ITEMS PAID AT SETTLEMENT.

800	ITEMS PAYABLE IN CONNECTION WITH LOAN;		1100	TITLE CHARGES	
801	Origination Fee @ % + $	$_____	1101	Closing or Escrow Fee	$_____
802	Discount Fee @ %+$	$_____	1102	Abstract or Title Search	$_____
803	Appraisal Fee	$_____	1103	Title Examination	$_____
804	Credit Report	$_____	1105	Document Preparation Fee	$_____
805	Lender's Inspection Fee	$_____	1106	Notary Fee	$_____
806	Mortgage Insurance Application Fee	$_____	1107	Attorney's Fee	$_____
807	Assumption Fee	$_____	1108	Title Insurance	$_____
808	Mortgage Broker Fee	$_____			$_____
810	Tax Related Service Fee	$_____			$_____
811	Application Fee	$_____			$_____
812	Commitment Fee	$_____			$_____
813	Lender's Rate Lock-In Fee	$_____			$_____
814	Processing Fee	$_____			$_____
815	Underwriting Fee	$_____			$_____
816	Wire Transfer Fee	$_____			$_____

900	ITEMS TO BE PAI DIN ADVANCE	;	1200	GOVERNMENT RECORDING AND TRANSFER CHARGES	
901	Interest for 1 days @ $13.78 day	$_____	1201	Recording Fee	$_____
902	Mortgage Insurance Premium	$_____	1202	City/County Tax/Stamps	$_____
903	Hazard Insurance Premium	$_____	1203	State Tax/Stamps	$_____
904	County Property Taxes	$_____	1205	Intangible Tax	$_____
905	Flood Insurance	$_____			$_____
		$_____			$_____

1000	RESERVES DEPOSITED WITH LENDER		1300	ADDITIONAL SETTLEMENT CHARGES	
1001	Hazard Ins 3 Mo @ $ 35 Per Mo	$_____	1201	Survey	$_____
1002	Mortgage Ins. Mo@$ Per Mo	$_____	1202	Pest Inspection	$_____
1004	Tax & Assmt. 7 Mo@$110 Per Mo	$_____	1203		$_____
1006	Flood Insurance	$_____	1205		$_____
		$_____		TOTAL ESTIMATED SETTLMENT CHARGES $_____	

S/B designates these costs to be paid by Seller / Broker   A designates those costs effecting APR

TOTAL ESTIMATED MONTHLY PAYMENT		TOTAL ESTIMATED FUNDS TO CLOSE	
Principal & Interest	$_____		
Real Estate Taxes	$_____	Down Payment	$_____
Hazard Insurance	$_____	Estimated Closing Costs (not financed)	$_____
Flood Insurance	$_____	Estimated Prepaid Items/Reserves	$_____
Mortgage Insurance	$_____	Total Paid Items (subtract)	$_____
Other	$_____	Other	$_____
TOTAL MONTHLY PAYMENT	$_____	CASH FROM BORROWER	$_____

2:7 Sample Form – Good Faith Estimate – HUD Release

The first section of the good faith estimate will define items that are payable in connection with the obtainment of the loan. The inclusions of each good faith estimate will vary slightly because the items charged to the borrower will be dependent on the structure of the loan being provided.

Always remember that alternative fees or 'junk fees' should remain similar for all borrowers regardless of their specific loan product or situation.

800 ITEMS PAYABLE IN CONNECTION WITH LOAN;		
801 Origination Fee @	% + $	$_____
802 Discount Fee @	% + $	$_____
803 Appraisal Fee		$_____
804 Credit Report		$_____
805 Lender's Inspection Fee		$_____
806 Mortgage Insurance Application Fee		$_____
807 Assumption Fee		$_____
808 Mortgage Broker Fee		$_____
810 Tax Related Service Fee		$_____
811 Application Fee		$_____
812 Commitment Fee		$_____
813 Lender's Rate Lock-In Fee		$_____
814 Processing Fee		$_____
815 Underwriting Fee		$_____
816 Wire Transfer Fee		$_____

2:8 Sample Form Extraction – Good Faith Estimate – HUD Release

800. ITEMS PAYABLE IN CONNECTION WITH THE LOAN

801. Origination Fee — The Origination Fee is usually known as a loan origination fee but is sometimes called a "point" or "points".

The origination fee covers the lenders administrative costs in processing the loan.

Often this fee is expressed as a percentage of the loan.

Generally, the buyer pays these fees. If the buyer and the seller negotiate a different method of payment, it will be defined within the sales agreement.

These points are charged on behalf of you or your branch. When working for a bank or a broker you have a negotiated commission schedule for all fees and points charged on the loan. You will also have a maximum limit to the points that you are allowed to charge.

You may charge points in two ways.

The first method of charging points is to wrap the points into the interest rate that you offer to the borrower. This will be discussed further in "pricing the loan".

The second method of charging points is as an up-front fee during the closing. Any up-front points will be reflected on the good faith estimate. If you do not include these fees within the good faith estimate, you will not be able to collect up-front fees on the loan.

A point is 1% of the loan amount.

802	Discount Fee	A discount fee is also called a loan discount point. A loan discount is a one-time charge imposed by the lender or broker to lower the rate at which the lender or broker would otherwise offer the loan.

This fee may vary.

In effect, the borrower is paying up front to reduce the overall monthly debt related to the loan. You may use the application of a discount fee to reduce the interest rate on a loan if the monthly payment exceeds the D. T. I. Ratio and the necessary funds are available to pay the discount fee.

This is also an excellent tool for your borrowers if the sellers have agreed to pay a set closing cost amount and the funds have not been utilized elsewhere.

These fees are paid to the lender.

803	Appraisal Fee	The Appraisal Fee covers the cost of the Appraisal.

The amount the appraisal fee is set by the appraisal company.

- The appraisal fee is often paid in advance.

  You will note this payment as paid in the details of transaction summary.

- The appraisal fee may be charged at the settlement.

These funds are paid to the Appraisal Company.

804	Credit Report	Any costs associated with the completion of the Credit Report will be disclosed on the good faith estimate.

Many lenders or brokers require the credit report charges be paid on all closed loans.

This amount is paid as a reimbursement to the lender.

The cost of the credit report is set regionally or by branch location. You should check with your branch manager for the amount.

At times, a lender may require the credit report fee be paid at the application meeting. In these cases, you will note the payment in the details of transaction summary as a fee paid in advance. |
| 805 | Lender's Inspection

borrower. | If the lender requires an inspection of the property for Underwriting purposes or another reason, the costs are the responsibility of the |
| 806 | Mortgage Insurance Application Fee | If Mortgage Insurance is necessary for the loan; any associated Application Fee should be included in the good faith estimate. This fee covers the processing of an application for mortgage insurance. |
| 807 | Assumption Fee Fee | If a loan is being assumed from the seller of the property, the lender assigning the loan to the new borrower may charge an Assumption.

This fee is charged when a buyer "assumes" or takes over the duty to pay the seller's existing mortgage loan |
| 808 | Mortgage Broker Fee | Some states or specific funding lenders require that all fees charged by the Broker be differentiated on the good faith estimate. .Mortgage Broker Fees are categorized with in this section of the good faith estimate. |

This separate disclosure helps to differentiate for the borrower the costs they are paying to the lending entity and the costs that they are paying for the Brokerage services.

810.	Tax Service Fee	Some lenders will use a service to verify the tax payment status of the property. Other lenders will rely on the settlement and closing company to perform this verification activity.

If a separate tax service entity is used to obtain the tax payment amounts and payment status, they will charge a fee for completing this action. The amount of the fee will vary by Service Company.

811	Application Fee	Some lenders or mortgage brokerage offices charge an up-front application fee.

This amount may include the credit report charges, appraisal fee, or additional costs as determined by the branch location.

- Often these charges are credited toward the closing in the event the loan is completed.

- These payments are typically kept to offset any costs incurred by the branch in the event the loan does not close.

The decision to charge an application fee is determined by a particular branch location or lender. You will want to verify whether your office charges an application fee, the amount of the fee, and how the fee will be allocated at loan closing.

You will want to be sure to note this payment in the details of transaction section of the 1003.

812	Commitment Fee estimate.	If your offices or the funding lender requires that the borrower pay a Commitment Fee, you must enter the amount into the good faith

This is often termed a "junk fee".

This is a fee charged by the lender in addition to points.

These fees are sometimes split per the negotiated commission schedule with the loan processor or loan officer.

813	Lender's Lock Rate Fee	Some lenders will charge a specific fee for the task of locking the interest

rate. This fee could be a service charge or may be a fee associated with the obtainment of a specific rate.

This fee is different from the discount points paid to buy down the interest rate.

814 Processing Fee

If your offices or the funding lender requires that the borrower pay a Processing Fee, you must enter the amount into the good faith estimate. This is often termed a "junk fee".

This is a fee charged by the lender in addition to points.

These fees are sometimes split per the negotiated commission schedule with the loan processor.

815 Underwriting Fee

If your office or the funding lender requires that the borrower pay an Underwriting Fee, you must enter the amount into the good faith estimate. This is often termed a "junk fee".

This is a fee charged by the lender in addition to points.

These fees are sometimes split per the negotiated commission schedule with the loan underwriter, loan officer, or loan processor but are more frequently credited entirely to the lender.

816 Wire Transfer Fee

Some lenders may charge a Wire Transfer Fee to cover the costs of wiring the required funds to close the loan.

This fee is a "buyer non-allowable fee" under some program guidelines. If a wire transfer fee is being charged on behalf of the branch or lender, you should incorporate the cost of this fee into the good faith estimate.

900 ITEMS TO BE PAI DIN ADVANCE	
901 Interest for ____ days @ $ ____ /day	$_____
902 Mortgage Insurance Premium	$_____
903 Hazard Insurance Premium	$_____
904 County Property Taxes	$_____
905 Flood Insurance	$_____

2:9 Sample Form Extraction – Good Faith Estimate – HUD Release

900   ITEMS REQUIRED BY THE LENDER TO BE PAID IN ADVANCE

Some fees related to the closing are recurring fees. These fees relate to costs associated with the carrying of the loan. The lender may require that the borrower pre-pay a specific quantity of these recurring fees as a condition of the loan closing. Some of these items would be accrued interest, mortgage insurance premiums, and homeowner's hazard insurance.

901   Interest

Lenders often require borrowers to pay the interest that accrues from the date of settlement or closing to the date that they will make the first monthly payment

This interest is prorated daily and based on the new loans interest rate.

902   Mortgage Insurance
        Premium

If mortgage insurance is a requirement of the loan being obtained, an up-front Premium may be charged. This premium may also be financed into the loan amount.

If the borrower pays the insured loan off within the first seven years, they may be entitled to a prorated refund of the fee.

You will include any up front premium in the good faith estimate and on the 1003.

903   Hazard Insurance
        Premium

Hazard insurance protects the borrower and the lender against loss due to fire, windstorm, and other hazards. .Lenders often require that the borrower to bring a paid-up first year's hazard insurance policy to the settlement or to pay for the first year's premium at settlement.

The premium amount should be included on the good faith estimate as a cost to close the loan. If the borrower pays this premium before closing, you will enter the amount of the payment into the pre-paid items on the 1003.

904   City Property Taxes

The city where the property is located may charge property taxes on real estate. The costs will be prorated between the buyer and the seller based on the closing date of the property and the negotiations included on the sales agreement. You will enter the borrower's estimated share of these costs into the good faith estimate.

905   Flood Insurance

If the lender requires flood insurance as a condition of the   loan, it is usually listed within the segment of the good faith estimate relating to items to be paid in advance. Many lenders will require that the borrower bring a fully paid policy illustrating flood coverage for the first year of homeownership as a condition of loan closing.

1004	County Property Tax	The County will assess property taxes on real estate.

The amount of property taxes collected will vary depending on the date of
closing, billing cycle of the taxes, and negotiations between the borrower and the seller.

The lender may require that the borrower escrow property taxes. Escrowing taxes means that the borrower pays a portion of the expected tax billing to the lender each month. The lender or servicer then holds these payments until the tax billing becomes due. The lender or servicer then uses the funds paid by the borrower to pay the tax bills related to the property.

1100 TITLE CHARGES	
1101 Closing or Escrow Fee	$_____
1102 Abstract or Title Search	$_____
1103 Title Examination	$_____
1105 Document Preparation Fee	$_____
1106 Notary Fee	$_____
1107 Attorney's Fee	$_____
1108 Title Insurance	$_____

2:10 Sample Form Extraction – Good Faith Estimate – HUD Release

1000   TITLE CHARGES

Any costs or charges associated with securing a clear title to the property and closing of the loan will be incorporated into the good faith estimate. Although these are not lender fees, lenders must provide a quote of the estimated costs of these items and services. These quotes may vary significantly. Title charges may cover a variety of services performed by title companies and others.

1101	Closing/Escrow Fee	A Closing or Escrow Fee is paid to the settlement agent or escrow holder. Responsibility for the payment of this fee should be negotiated between the seller and the buyer and will appear on the sales agreement provided to you by either the real estate agent or the borrower.
1102		Abstract/Title Search Any fees required for the completion of the

Abstract or Title Search on the property will be charged by the Title Company to the borrower.

The payment of these fees may be negotiated as part of the sales agreement between the borrower and the seller.

You can contact the closing company handling the settlement to obtain a figure for this field.

1105	Document Preparation Fee	Any cost charged by the title company for the service of preparing all of the closing documents not provided by the funding company will be entered into the good faith estimate under Document Preparation Fee.

Lender or Funding Company charges for document preparation costs will be included within a different section of the good faith estimate.

1106	Notary Fee parties	The charge incurred for the notary who verifies the signatures of all

on the documents during the closing should be included within the good faith estimate.

You can contact the closing company handling the settlement to obtain a figure for this field.

1107	Attorney's Fee portion	In the event that the services of an attorney are required during any

of the loan application, processing, or closing activity, the costs charged by the attorney for these services should be entered into the good faith estimate.

The attorney will provide you with an estimate of his or her charges for the requested services.

1200 GOVERNMENT RECORDING AND TRANSFER CHARGES

1201 Recording Fee	$_____
1202 City/County Tax/Stamps	$_____
1203 State Tax/Stamps	$_____
1205 Intangible Tax	$_____

2:11 Sample Form Extraction – Good Faith Estimate – HUD Release

1200   GOVERNMENT RECORDING AND TRANSFER

Fees charged at the courthouse where the mortgage documents are filed will be allocated in association with the loan. The borrower typically pays these costs, but you should refer to the sales agreement to ensure that no other negotiations relating to the payment of these fees has been made. These fees are payable to the government.

1201   Recording fee   A recording fee is the amount charged for the recording of each item
        that

                              must be filed within the public records system.

                              These items are filed for the protection of both the borrower and the
                              lender.

                              Recording costs vary depending on the region where the recording will
                              occur. You will want to verify the costs with your Title Company,
                              courthouse, or branch manager.

1202   City/County Tax
        Stamps   City and County Taxes and Stamps are the taxes assessed when
        real

                              property is transferred within a city and county.

                              Different areas have different tax costs. You will want to verify this
                              figure with your Title Company, courthouse, or branch manager.

1203   State Tax Stamps   State Tax Stamps are the state required taxes involved with the transfer
        of

                              the property.

                              Different states have different tax costs and you will want to verify this
                              figure with your Title Company, courthouse, or branch manager.

1300   ADDITIONAL SETTLEMENT CHARGES:

Any additional charges incurred during the loan processes that have not been addressed previously will be explained and entered within the final area of the good faith estimate

1301   Survey   Many lenders accept a survey affidavit from the Title Company as
                              verification of the property location and boundary lines.

                              If a survey must be performed for the property to clear underwriting,
                              these charges are negotiated as paid by the buyer or the seller of the
                              property and the figure is paid to the Survey Company at settlement.

1302	Pest Inspections	Pest Inspections are required by some loan programs and are requested in some cases by the buyer

The payment for these fees is negotiated on the Real Estate Sales Agreement.

These payments are paid to the inspection provider based on a billing presented at the closing table.

1303   Flood Certification

A Flood Certification or verification that the property is not in a flood plain may be requested by underwriting.

If the flood certification is completed through a service retained by underwriting, the costs of the certification are paid to the lender at the time of closing and the lender pays the certification service.

If another certification service is used to verify the flood status of the property, the name of the service will be entered into the good faith estimate and the charges imposed by the service included.

Payment to the service provider may be made during the loan process or as part of the settlement process. You should enter the applicable details into the good faith estimate.

1304   Courier Fees

Courier Fees may be charged by either the funding company or closing company for the transfer of documents via courier.

You will want to check with your closing provider and your branch manager to determine if this fee is commonly charged.

KENNEY

Lender:	Sales Price:
Address:	Base Loan Amount:
	Total Loan Amount:
Applicant(s):	Interest Rate:
	Type of Loan:
Property Address:	Preparation Date:
	Loan Number

The information provided below reflects estimates of the charges which you are likely to incur at the settlement of your loan. The fees   listed are estimates – actual charges may be more or less. Your transaction may not involve a fee for every item listed. THE NUMBERS LISTED BESIDE THE ESTIMATES GENERALLY CORRESPOND TO THE NUMBERED LINES CONTAINED THE HUD-1 OR HUD-1A SETTLEMENT STATEMENT WHICH YOU WILL BE RECEIVEING AT THE SETTLEMENT. THE HUD-1 OR HUD-1A SETTLEMENT STATEMENT WILL SHOW YOU THE ACTUAL COST FOR ITEMS PAID AT SETTLEMENT.

800	ITEMS PAYABLE IN CONNECTION WITH LOAN;		1100	TITLE CHARGES	
801	Origination Fee @ % + $	$2550.00	1101	Closing or Escrow Fee	$ 295.00
802	Discount Fee @ %+$	$	1102	Abstract or Title Search	$
803	Appraisal Fee	$ 275.00	1103	Title Examination	$
804	Credit Report	$ 50.00	1105	Document Preparation Fee	$
805	Lender's Inspection Fee	$	1106	Notary Fee	$ 35.00
806	Mortgage Insurance Application Fee	$	1107	Attorney's Fee	$
807	Assumption Fee	$	1108	Title Insurance	$ 618.75
808	Mortgage Broker Fee	$			$
810	Tax Related Service Fee	$ 98.00			$
811	Application Fee	$			$
812	Commitment Fee	$			$
813	Lender's Rate Lock-In Fee	$ 200.00			$
814	Processing Fee	$ 250.00			$
815	Underwriting Fee	$ 400.00			$
816	Wire Transfer Fee	$			$

900	ITEMS TO BE PAI DIN ADVANCE ;		1200	GOVERNMENT RECORDING AND TRANSFER CHARGES	
901	Interest for 1 days @ $13.78 day	$ 13.78	1201	Recording Fee	$ 33.50
902	Mortgage Insurance Premium	$	1202	City/County Tax/Stamps	$ 80.00
903	Hazard Insurance Premium	$ 420.00	1203	State Tax/Stamps	$ 80.00
904	County Property Taxes	$1320.00	1205	Intangible Tax	$
905	Flood Insurance	$			$
		$			$

1000	RESERVES DEPOSITED WITH LENDER		1300	ADDITIONAL SETTLEMENT CHARGES	
1001	Hazard Ins 3 Mo @ $ 35 Per Mo	$ 105.00	1201	Survey	$
1002	Mortgage Ins. Mo@$ Per Mo	$	1202	Pest Inspection	$
1004	Tax & Assmt. 7 Mo@$110 Per Mo	$ 770.00	1203		$
1006	Flood Insurance	$	1205		$
		$		TOTAL ESTIMATED SETTLMENT CHARGES	$

S/B designates these costs to be paid by Seller / Broker   A designates those costs effecting APR

TOTAL ESTIMATED MONTHLY PAYMENT		TOTAL ESTIMATED FUNDS TO CLOSE	
Principal & Interest	$ 616.00		
Real Estate Taxes	$ 110.00	Down Payment	$
Hazard Insurance	$ 35.00	Estimated Closing Costs (not financed)	$7743.03
Flood Insurance	$	Estimated Prepaid Items/Reserves	$
Mortgage Insurance	$	Total Paid Items (subtract)	$
Other	$	Other	$
TOTAL MONTHLY PAYMENT	$ 761.00	CASH FROM BORROWER	$

APPROVED SERVICE PROVIDER LIST

Some mortgage lenders will use specific service providers when completing the processing and closing of a loan application. If the mortgage lender uses a specific service provider and the borrower will be responsible for the billing that is incurred as a result of this use, the lender must provide a disclosure to the borrower detailing this use so that the borrower has the opportunity to make an informed decision applicable to the costs that they will incur.

APPROVED SERVICE PROVIDER LIST

Addendum to the standard "Good Faith Estimate" of Settlement Costs

_____ requires the use of certain providers in the processing and settlement of your loan. These providers are chosen from an approved list and we require that you pay for all portions of the services provided from these providers. The costs of these services are based on the charges of these providers or industry standards. Please refer to your attached Good Faith Estimate form for an estimate of each proposed charge. The following providers have been repeatedly used for the designated services within the last 12 months.

1.   CREDIT REPORTING AGENCIES:

2.   APPRAISAL SERVICES:

3.   PRIVATE MORTGAGE INSURANCE PROVIDERS:

4.   OTHER:

I/we acknowledge that we received a copy of this notice:

_____   _____
Borrower Signature   Date

_____   _____
Co-Borrower Signature   Date

2:12 Sample Form– Approved Service Provider List – HUD Release

RATE LOCK OR FLOAT OPTION

The borrower must complete a rate lock or float option form. This form specifies the borrower's determination as to whether they wish to lock in the offered interest rate now or wait on the chance that the interest rate will change for the better during the loan processing stage.

The upper section of the form should provide identifying details relating to the borrower, the property, and the loan. The form will have two areas. The borrower should complete and sign the area that relates to their choice.

If they wish to lock in the currently offered interest rate, they will complete the RATE LOCK section of the form. The rate lock section will show the offered rate, any points associated with the obtainment of this rate, and the number of days that the rate lock offer is applicable.

The borrower will sign and date the form to illustrate their acceptance of the offered rate and terms.

If the borrower wishes to wait to lock the rate in the hopes that the market will improve thus improving the interest rate that they can obtain, the borrower will complete the DO NOT LOCK section of the form by signing and dating the applicable area.

The borrower should receive a copy of the completed rate lock form.

RATE LOCK/RATE FLOAT OPTION

Loan Amount $_____

Property Address   _____

City, State, Zip   _____

This is to certify that I DO want to exercise my interest rate lock option at this time.

A.   My guaranteed interest rate will be ____%.

B.   The total points paid at settlement will not exceed _____. This total does not include settlement costs such as title insurance, homeowners insurance, transfer taxes, etc.

C.

D.   This agreement will end _____ days from today. This date is called the ending date.

ACKNOWLEDGEMENT

_____   _____
Signed   Date

This is to certify that I DO NOT want to exercise my interest rate lock option at this time.

A.   I understand that my lender cannot predict interest rate changes.

B.   If I want to obtain an interest rate commitment in the future, I may do so at any time up to ___ days before the closing of my mortgage loan.

C.   I understand that I must sign an interest rate lock-in agreement to obtain a guaranteed interest rate lock.

D.   I understand that it is my responsibility to advise the lender of my desire to obtain interest rate commitment.

ACKNOWLEDGEMENT

_____   _____
Signed   Date

_____   _____
Signed   Date

2:13 Sample Form– Rate Lock / Float Option – HUD Release

AFFILIATED BUSINESS ARRANGEMENT NOTICE

If the lender has a business arrangement or interest in one of the service providers associated with the loan process or closing, the lender must give the borrower notice of this arrangement or interest. An Affiliated Business Arrangement Notice should be provided to the borrower, and a signature obtained that acknowledges the borrowers understanding of this business arrangement or interest. The borrower should receive a copy of this notice.

Affiliated Business Arrangement Notice

This is to give you notice that   has a business relationship with
(Describe the nature of the relationship between the referring party and the provider(s) including percentage of
ownership interest, if applicable). Because of this relationship, this referral may provide a financial or other benefit.

(A.) Set forth below is the estimated charge or range of charges for the settlement services listed. You are NOT
required to use the listed provider(s) as a condition for (settlement of your loan) (or) (purchase, sale or refinance
of) the subject property. THERE ARE FREQUENTLY OTHER SETTLEMENT SERVICE PROVIDERS
AVAILABLE WITH SIMILAR SERVICES. YOU ARE FREE TO SHOP AROUND TO DETERMINE THAT
YOU ARE RECEIVING THE BEST RATE FOR THESE SERVICES.

_____

_____

(B.) Set forth below is the estimated charge or range of charges for the settlement services of an attorney, credit
reporting agency, or real estate appraiser that we, as your lender, will require you to use, as a condition of your
loan on this property, to represent our interests in this transaction.

_____

_____

ACKNOWLEDGMENT

I/we have read this disclosure form and understand that (referring party) is referring me/us to purchase the above
described settlement service(s) and may receive a financial benefit as a result of this referral.

_____   _____

2:14 Sample Form– Affiliated Business Arrangement Notice – HUD Release

MAILING ADDRESS CONFIRMATION

The lender who provides the funds for the closing will often ask the borrower to sign a statement confirming their mailing address and understanding of the monthly payment dictated through the mortgage and note documents. This statement will

- Detail the correspondence information of the borrower

- State the monthly payment breakdown specifics including breakdown information for PMI, school and county taxes, insurance premiums and any reserves required under the mortgage agreement

- Define any mortgage servicing information known to the mortgage lender at the time of closing

- Detail the mailing address and other contact information of the mortgage lender

The borrower will be asked to review all of the entries on this document and confirm a receipt of a copy of the statement. The mailing address and payment confirmation is a snapshot of all of the data pertaining to the loan that was included on the previous pages and it is critical that you ensure the borrower receives a copy of this statement in their closing package.

KENNEY

MAILING ADDRESS CONFIRMATION / PAYMENT LETTER

From:

Re: Loan #   *** IMPORTANT, PLEASE READ THROUGHOULY ***
        Property Address

To:

Dear Homeowner:

A.   All mortgage servicing correspondence will be mailed to the above referenced property address. In order to ensure proper
        receipt of all mortgage servicing notifications (i.e. monthly statement, Q&A booklets, etc.) please indicate the correct
        mailing address if it is different from the property address. The address to mail payments and the phone number to call
        for customer service are listed below.

        Please indicate (X):

        ( )   The property address is correct as referenced above and should be used for correspondence.

        ( )   The proper mailing address is: _____

                                                   _____

B..   The monthly payments on the above loan are to begin on   , and will continue monthly until

        Your monthly payment will consist of the following:

        MONTHLY PAYMENT ....$_____
        MMI/PMI INSRUANCE .... _____
        RESERVE FOR COUNTY TAXES .... _____
        RESERVE FOR HAXARD INSURANCE................................... _____
        RESERVE FOR FLOOD INSURANCE.................................... _____
        RESERVE FOR CITY TAXES..._____
        RESERVE FOR ANNUAL ASSESSMENT................................_____
        RESERVE FOR SCHOOL TAXES......................................._____
        _____....................._____
                            TOTAL MONTHLY PAYMENTS.........$_____

*** Please be aware that if you have an impound account, you may see a change in your initial monthly payment figure due to
information available after the closing of your loan.

                        Engages the services of   as its servicer. You will be receiving a billing
notice from   within two weeks of your loan funding.   has the right to
collect your payments and this in no way affects the terms and conditions of the mortgage instruments, other than the terms directly
related to the servicing of your loan. If you do not receive a payment booklet or have other questions about the servicing of your
loan, please call:

2:15 Sample Form – Mailing Address Confirmation Letter – HUD Release

MORTGAGE SERVICING TRANSFER NOTIFICATION

In today's market, mortgage-servicing rights are often bought and sold. THE REAL ESTATE SETTLEMENT PROCEDURES ACT provides certain rights regarding the servicing of the mortgage and escrow accounts.

The servicing of a mortgage loan means the continued collection of payments, management of escrow, and the handling of all post close activity relating to the mortgage loan until the loan is paid in full.

Many lenders will sell the servicing rights of a mortgage to another company after the closing of the transaction. At the closing, information pertaining to how often the mortgage lender transfers servicing rights, the handling of such a transfer, and the effects of such transfer on the buyer will be disclosed. It is important that the buyer understand these documents and receive a copy of all documents so that they may refer to the inclusions if, at some point, the loan servicing is transferred.

If a loan is transferred to a new servicer, the loan servicer is required to notify the borrower in writing at least 15 days before the servicing of the loan is transferred to a new servicer.

The notice must include.

- The effective date of the transfer

- The date the new servicer will begin accepting payments.

- The name, address, and toll-free or collect call telephone number for the new servicer.

- Information concerning the continuance of any optional insurance, such as mortgage life or disability insurance

- A statement that the transfer of the loan servicing does not affect any term or condition of the mortgage documents other than the terms directly related to the servicing of the loan.

- An explanation that the payment may not be treated as late during the 60-day period beginning on the effective date of the transfer if it is mistakenly sent it to the old mortgage servicer instead of the new one.

Mortgage Servicing Disclosure

NOTICE TO MORTGAGE LOAN APPLICATNS: THE RIGHT TO COLLECT YOUR MORTGAGE LOAN PAYMENTS MAY BE TRANSFERRED. FEDERAL LAW GIVES YOU CERTAIN RELATED RIGHTS. READ THIS STATEMTN AND SIGN IT ONLY IF YOU UNDERSTAND ITS CONTENTS.

Because you are applying for a mortgage loan covered by the Real Estate Settlement Procedures Act (RESPA), you have certain rights under that Federal law. This statement tells you about those rights. It also tells you what the chances are that the servicing for this loan may be transferred to a different loan servicer. "Servicing" refers to collecting your principal, interest and escrow account payments, if any. If your loan servicer changes, certain procedures must be followed. This statement generally explains those procedures.

Transfer Practices and Requirements
If the servicing of your loan is assigned, sold or transferred to a new servicer you must be given notice of that transfer. The present loan servicer must send you notice in writing of the assignment, sale, or transfer of the servicing not less than 15 days before the effective date of the transfer. The present servicer and the new servicer may combine this information in one notice so long as the notice is sent to you within 15 days before the effective date of the transfer. The 15-day period is not applicable if a notice of prospective transfer is provided to you at settlement. The law allows a delay in the time (not more than 30 days after a transfer) for servicers to notify you under certain limited circumstances, when your servicer is changed abruptly. This exception applies only if your servicer is fired for cause, is in bankruptcy proceedings, or is involved in a conservatorship or receivership initiated by a Federal Agency.

Notices must contain certain information. They must contain the effective date of the transfer of the servicing of your loan to the new servicer, the name, address and toll-free or collect call telephone number of the new servicer, and toll-free or collect call telephone numbers of a person or department for both your present servicer and your new servicer to answer your questions about the transfer of servicing. During the 60-day period following the effective date of the transfer of the loan servicing, a loan payment received by your old servicer before its due date may not be treated by the new servicer as late and a late fee may not be imposed on you.

Complaint Resolution
Section 5 of RESPA gives you certain consumer rights *whether or not your loan servicing is transferred*. If you send a qualified written request to your loan servicer concerning the servicing of your loan, your servicer must provide you with a written acknowledgement within 20 business days of receipt of your request. A "qualified written request" is a written correspondence other than notice on payment coupon or other payment medium supplied by the servicer that includes your name and account number and your reasons for the request. Not later than 60 Business Days after receiving your request, your servicer must make any appropriate corrections to your account or must provide you with a written clarification regarding any dispute. During this 60-Business Day period, your servicer may not provide any information to a consumer reporting agency concerning any overdue payment related to such period or qualified written request.

A business day is any day excluding public holidays, State or Federal, Saturday or Sunday.

Damages and Costs
Section 6 of RESPA also provides for damages and costs for individuals in circumstances where servicers are shown to have violated the requirements of that section.

Servicing Transfer Estimated by Lender

1.   The following is the best estimate of what will happen to the servicing of your loan:

        We may assign, sell, or transfer the servicing of your loan sometime while the loan is outstanding. We are able to service your loan and we presently intend to service your loan.

2.   For all mortgage loans that we make in the 12-month period after your mortgage loan is funded, we estimate that the percentage of mortgage loans for which we will transfer servicing is between:

        ___ and ___%

         This is only our best estimate and it is not binding. Business conditions or other circumstances may affect

3.   This is our record of transferring the servicing of mortgage loans we have made in the past:

        Year   Percentage of Loans Transferred

2:16 Sample Form – Mortgage Servicing Disclosure – HUD Release

RIGHT TO RECEIVE A COPY OF THE APPRAISAL

When an appraisal has been conducted as a part of the transaction, the borrower has a right to obtain a copy of said appraisal if they have paid for the completion.

- The appraisal will often be delivered directly to the lender during the course of the loan process.

- The loan processor should provide instructions to the buyer on how to obtain a copy of the appraisal if they desire one at or before the settlement meeting.

- These instructions must be signed and witnessed during the closing process.

NOTICE REGARDING YOUR
UNIFORM RESIDENTIAL APPRAISAL REPORT

You are advised that you have the right, under the Equal Credit Opportunity Act, to obtain a copy of your *Uniform Residential Appraisal Report*.

If you wish a copy, please write us at the address shown below. We must hear from you no later than 90 days after we notify you about the action taken on your credit application or you withdraw your application.

Please send your written request to:

In your letter, give the following information:

     Loan or application number (if known)

     Date of application

     Name(s) of loan applicant(s)

     Property address

     Current mailing address

A copy of your Uniform Residential Appraisal Report shall be mailed to you within 30 days after receipt of your request.

2:17 Sample Form – Right to Receive a Copy of Appraisal – HUD Release

RIGHT OF RECISSION/RIGHT TO CANCEL

Some transactions must include a RIGHT for the borrower to rescind or CANCEL the loan after the closing date.

Any credit transaction that involves a security interest in the borrower's primary residence must provide the borrower with the right to rescind the transaction.

RIGHT OF RECISSION LENDER RESPONSABLITY

The lender has certain responsibilities that help to protect these rights.

- Lenders are required to provide two copies of the right to cancel or rescind to the borrower.

- The notice must be on a separate document that identifies the rescission period available to the borrower.

- The notice must clearly disclose the fact that the borrower's primary residence will be held as a security instrument because of the transaction.

- The notice must state the borrower's right to rescind or cancel the transaction.

- The notice must state how the borrower may exercise the right to rescind or cancel.

- The notice must designate the address of the lender or the place of business to which the rescission or cancellation must be delivered.

- The borrower will receive a refund of all money or property provided to the lender within twenty days of delivery of the decision to rescind or cancel the transaction.

RIGHT OF RESCISSION BORROWER RESPONSIBILITY

The borrower also has certain responsibilities with regard to the right to cancel a credit transaction.

- In order to notify the lender of the decision to rescind or cancel the transaction the borrower must notify the lender of the decision in writing.

- The decision must be delivered to the lender by mail, telegram or other communication available, which allows for written delivery of the signature of the borrower.

- The borrower may exercise the right to rescind or cancel the transaction until midnight on the third day of the transaction.

- When more than one borrower in a transaction has the right to rescind or cancel the exercise of the right of rescission or cancellation by one borrower shall be binding upon all borrowers.

- When a borrower rescinds or cancels the transaction the security interest resulting from the transaction becomes void.

- The borrower will receive a refund of all money or property provided to the lender within twenty days of delivery of the decision to rescind or cancel the transaction.

- The borrower may waive the right to rescind by completing the applicable notice.

NOTICE OF RIGHT TO CANCEL

Your Right to Cancel

You are entering a transaction that will result in a mortgage on your home. You have a legal right under Federal Law to cancel this transaction without cost until midnight of the third business day after, whichever of the following events occurs last

    (1.)   the date of the closing of the transaction

    (2.)   the date you received your Truth in Lending disclosure

    (3.)   the date you received this notice of your right to cancel

If you cancel the transaction, the mortgage is also canceled. Within 20 calendar days after we receive your notice we must take the steps necessary to reflect the fact that the mortgage on your house has been cancelled, and we must return to you any money or property you have given to us or to anyone else in connection with this transaction. You may keep any money or property we have given you until we have completed the items mentioned above, but you must return the money or property upon completion of the described actions. If it is impractical or unfair for you to return the property, you must offer its reasonable value. You may offer to return the property at your home or at the location of the property. Money must be returned to the address below. If we do not take possession of the money or property within 20 calendar days of your offer, you may keep it without further obligation.

How to Cancel

If you decide to cancel this transaction you may do so by notifying

_____

_____

You may use any written statement that is signed and dated by you and states your intention to cancel, or you may use this notice by dating and signing below. Keep one copy of this notice because it contains important information about your rights.

If you cancel by mail, you must send the notice no later than midnight of_____, 20___ (or midnight of the third business day following the latest of the events listed above.) If you send or deliver your written notice to cancel in some other manner, it must be delivered to the above address no later than that time.

2:18 Sample Form –Notice of Right to Cancel – HUD Release

SETTLEMENT STATEMENT

The settlement statement is the statement that itemizes all closing costs payable at the closing or settlement meeting.

The settlement statement will contain details derived from the good faith estimate, the sales agreement, payoff and billing information, and other specific figures supplied to the closing agent's office.

You will typically not be responsible for the completion of the settlement statement, but you should understand the inclusions and gain the ability to compare the financial details of the settlement statement to the loan specifics offered to the borrower. It will be a part of your function to review the settlement statement prior to the settlement meeting. You should confirm that the numbers included match the loan strategy and details that the borrower expects.

The borrower's portion of the settlement statement should mirror the initial Good Faith Estimate.

The settlement statement is the statement that itemizes all closing costs payable at the closing or settlement meeting.

The seller's portion of the settlement statement breaks down all items on the seller's behalf. Included in the seller's portion will be:

- Any liens or mortgages that must be paid to secure a clear title to the property

- Any seller concession toward the buyers closing costs (as negotiated in the Sales Agreement) and any additional charges for which the seller is responsible.

- Any prorated items the seller has agreed to pay as negotiated in the sales agreement.

- Any other costs the seller has incurred that must be paid at the closing table.

You will wish to review the seller's portion to ensure that any concessions, assumed loans, or costs the seller has agreed to pay as part of the purchase negotiations are correctly debited from the seller and credited to your borrower. An error in the allocation of concessions or costs will affect the figures on the borrower's side of the settlement statement.

The settlement statement contains the final figures pertaining to the loan. It is your duty to review the settlement statement before the closing meeting. You should confirm that all of the details set forth on the settlement statement are in agreement with the loan program structured for the borrower.

Page one section 100 will contain the total of all costs involved with the loan process. These will include:

- The sales price

- Any Settlement charges allocated to the borrower.

- Any pro-rated taxes due from the borrower

Section 200 will contain all amounts, which are paid on behalf of the borrower. These will include:

- Any deposit or earnest money the borrower paid at the time of the Sales Agreement negotiation.

- Any additional deposits or payments made by the borrower in the course of the loan processing.

- The loan amount as negotiated with the lender.

- Any assumed loans the borrower is taking.

- Any seller financing as negotiated at the time of the sales agreement.

- Any closing costs to be paid by the seller as negotiated at the time of the Sales Agreement.

- Any additional adjustments that the Title Company has determined must be made to the finances of the package.

The figures will be calculated, taking the amount paid on behalf of the borrower, and the amount due from the borrower to determine the exact figure the borrower is required to bring to the closing table.

You should review the final settlement statement to confirm that all of the figures match the loan as it has been structured and that the cash to or from the borrower matches the estimate of charges on the initial good faith estimate. A very small amount of change is expected due to the pro-rata of exact charges. However, if the figures vary greatly from the initial estimate, the Settlement Statement will need to be reviewed with more care to determine exactly where the error has occurred.

Page two of the settlement statement contains a more detailed breakdown of the charges included in the section titled settlement charges to borrower. The fees and costs being charged on the loan will be included in this section. These figures will mirror the good faith estimate making an error relatively simple to find.

Upon confirming that the Settlement Statement is in agreement with the Good Faith Estimate and the planned structuring of the loan, you should inform the Settlement Company that the Settlement Statement is approved. The closing can then go forward.

F. Type of Loan				
1__ FHA 2 __ FmHA 3__ Conv 4 __ VA 5 __ Conv Ins	6. File Number:		7. Loan Number:	8. Mortgage Insurance Case Number

G. Note: This form is furnished to give you a statement of actual settlement costs. Amounts paid to and by the settlement agent are shown. Items marked "(P&C)" were paid outside the closing; they are shown here for informational purposes and are not included in the totals.

D. Name & Address of Borrower.	E. Name & Address of Seller	F. Name & Address of Lender
G. Property Location	H. Settlement Agent Place of Settlement:	I. Settlement Date

J. Summary of Borrower's Transaction		**K. Summary of Seller's Transaction**	
100. Gross Amount Due From Borrower		**400. Gross Amount Due To Seller**	
101. Contract Sales Price		401. Contact Sales Price	
102. Personal Property		402. Personal Property	
103. Settlement Charges to borrower (line 1400)		403.	
104.		404.	
105.		405.	
Adjustments for items paid by seller in advance		Adjustments for items paid by seller in advance	
106. City / Town Taxes for		406. City / Town Taxes for	
107. County Taxes for		407. County Taxes for	
108. Assessments for		408. Assessments for	
109.		409.	
110.		410.	
111.		411.	
112.		412.	
120. Gross Amount Due From Borrower		**420. Gross Amount Due To Seller**	
200. Amounts Paid By Or In Behalf Of Borrower		**500. Reductions In Amount Due To Seller**	
201. Deposit or earnest money		501. Excess deposit (see instructions)	
202. Principal amount of new loan(s)		502. Settlement charges to seller (line 1400)	
203. Existing loan(s) take subject to		503. Existing loan(s) taken subject to	
204.		504. Payoff of first mortgage loan	
205.		505. Pay off of second mortgage loan	
206.		506.	
207.		507.	
208.		508.	
209.		509.	
Adjustments for items unpaid by seller		Adjustments for items unpaid by seller	
210. City / Town Taxes for		510. City / Town Taxes for	
211. County Taxes for		511. County Taxes for	
212. Assessments for		512. Assessments for	
213.		513.	
214.		514.	
215.		515.	
216.		516.	
217.		517.	
218.		518.	
219.		519.	
220. Total Paid By/For Borrower		**520. Total Reduction Amount Due Seller**	
300. Cash At Settlement From/To Borrower		**600. Cash at Settlement To/From Seller**	
301. Gross amount due from borrower (line 120)		601. Gross amount due to seller (line 420)	
302. Less amounts paid by/for borrower (line 220)	( )	602. Less reductions in amt due seller (line 520)	( )

2:19 Sample Form – HUD 1 Settlement Statement Page 1 – HUD Release

	Paid From Borrowers Funds at Settlement	Paid From Seller's Funds at Settlement
700. Total Sales/Brokers commission based on price $ @ %		
Division of Commission (line 700) as follows:		
701. $ to		
702. $ to		
703 Commission paid at Settlement		
704.		
800. Items Payable in Connection with Loan		
801. Loan Origination Fee %		
802. Loan Discount %		
803. Appraisal Fee to		
804. Credit Report to		
805. Lender's Inspection Fee		
806. Mortgage Insurance Application Fee to		
807. Assumption Fee		
808.		
809.		
810.		
811.		
900. Items Required By Lender To Be Paid In Advance		
901. Interest from to @$ / day		
902. Mortgage Insurance Premium for months to		
903. Hazard Insurance Premium for years to		
904.		
905.		
1000. Reserves Deposited With Lender		
1001. Hazard Insurance months @$ per month		
1002. Mortgage Insurance months @$ per month		
1003. City Property Taxes months @$ per month		
1004. County Property Taxes months @$ per month		
1005. Annual Assessments months @$ per month		
1006. months @$ per month		
1007. months @$ per month		
1008. months @$ per month		
1100. Title Charges		
1101. Settlement or closing fee to		
1102. Abstract or title search to		
1103. Title examination to		
1104. Title insurance binder to		
1105. Document preparation to		
1106. Notary fees to		
1107. Attorney's fees to		
(includes above items numbers:)		
1108. Title Insurance to		
(includes above items numbers:)		
1109. Lender's coverage $		
1110. Owner's coverage $		
1111.		
1112.		
1200. Government Recording and Transfer Charges		
1201. Recording fees: Deed $: Mortgage $: Releases $		
1202. City/county tax/stamps: Deed $: Mortgage $		
1203. State tax/stamps: Deed $: Mortgage $		
1204.		
1205.		
1300. Additional Settlement Charges		
1301. Survey to		
1302. Pest Inspection to		
1303.		
1304.		
1305.		
1400. Total Settlement Charges (enter on lines 103, Section J and 502, Section K)		

2:20 Sample Form – HUD1 Settlement Statement Page 2 – HUD Release

ESCROW ACCOUNT DISCLOSURE STATEMENT

When the loan is being structured, one element that must be considered is whether to impound property tax and insurance payments or to allow the borrower to pay these billings themselves as they come due.

- At times, the buyer will pay a portion of these bills each month as part of their monthly payment.

- The funds will then be placed into an escrow account until the billings become due.

- The lender then uses the payments made by the borrower throughout the year to makes payment for these billings.

- At other times, the buyer may agree to pay the billings as they become due.

This is known as impounding, not impounding, escrowing, or not escrowing payments.

Whichever method is chosen, a document will often be presented at closing that details the choices, handling and confirms the actions required of each party. You must obtain the proper signature on these documents, as the payment of such billings can be critical to maintaining the rights of the parties in the transaction.

BORROWER(S):

PROPERTY ADDRES:

NON IMPOUND NOTICE

I DO UNDERSTAND THAT THE LENDER FOR THIS MORTGAGE WILL NOT IMPOUND FOR REAL ESTATE TAXES AND HOMEOWNERS INSURANCE COVERAGE ON THE ABOVE REFERENCED ACCOUNT.

THE MONTHLY PAYMENT I WILL BE MAKING ONLY COVERS PRINCIPAL AND INTEREST ON THE LOAN.

I AM FULLY RESPONSIBLE TO PAY FOR REAL ESTATE TAXES AND HOMEOWNERS INSURACE POLICY PREMIUMS WHEN THEY BECOME PAYABLE.

2:21 Sample Form – Non Impound Notice – HUD Release

INITIAL ESCROW ACCOUNT DISCLOSURE STATEMENT

Borrower Name and Address	Lender's Name and Address
Loan No.	Telephone No.

___ Your mortgage payment for the coming year will be $_____ of which $_____ will be for principal and interest and $_____ will go into your escrow account.

___ Your first monthly mortgage payment for the coming year will be $_____ of which $_____ will be for principal and interest and $_____ will go into your escrow account.

The terms of your loan may result in changes to the principal and interest payments during the year.

This is an estimate of activity in your escrow account during the coming year based on payments anticipated to be made from your account.

Month/ Payment No.	Payments to Escrow Acct.	Payment from Escrow Acct.	Description	Escrow Acct. Balance

Please keep this statement for comparison with the actual activity in your account at the end of the escrow accounting computation year. Cushion selected by the servicer is $_____.

2:22 Sample Form – Initial Escrow Account Disclosure Statement – HUD Release

PRO-RATA CALCULATIONS

The function of completing the pro-rata calculations will often be assigned to the title agent in charge of the loan file or to the closing agent who works for the mortgage lender. While the completion of the final pro-rata calculations will typically not be a part of your functions, you should gain an understanding of the methodology behind these calculations. You will need apply these figures in your functions and when reviewing the good faith estimate and HUD 1.

Prorating allows for the buyer and seller to split the costs and income related to the property fairly according to the term of ownership. These prorations may be based on the date of closing or another date as negotiated within the sales contract.

Items subject to pro-rata may include

- Real estate taxes

- Homeowner's insurance premiums

- Accrued interest on assumed loans

- Rents received on income producing property

- Other income received from an income producing property

- Expenses incurred on an income producing property

- Oil or other fuel tank filling costs

- Any utility billing for any utility not turned off and paid in full prior to the date of closing

- Any other negotiated matter.

These are the most common items subject to pro ration negotiations, but as each transaction is different, the items to be pro-rated may be different. It is important that any financial matter that may be subject to a split between the buyer and the seller be negotiated, in writing, in the sales agreement or another document. This written negotiation ensures that all parties understand the income and expenses that may be assessed. The written negotiations also provide the settlement company with the information necessary to prorate the applicable items according to the party's wishes. You will enter an estimate of any pro-rated items in the good faith estimate before you provide the estimate to the borrower.

KENNEY

30-DAY MONTH

It is customary to complete the pro ration calculations based on a 30-day month rather than altering the figures to the exact number of days within the closing month. This 30-day month is used when prorating

- Mortgage Interest

- Property Taxes

- Water Bills

- Insurance Premiums

- And other items as determined by the specific transaction.

If the use of the customary 30-day month creates a significant financial impact on either the buyer or the seller, they can agree to prorate using the exact number of days in the applicable month or to use the 365-day year to find the daily pro ration calculation rate. Any negotiation of this sort will be incorporated into the sales contract or written as an addendum to the sales contract.

REAL ESTATE TAXES

To understand how pro-rata calculations affect the financial figures associated with the closing, we will define the figures for an example real estate property tax calculation.
Real estate property tax pro-rations are common to nearly every real estate transaction. The date basis for the calculation will depend on

- The number of times taxes are assessed per year.

- The due date of each tax billing cycle

- The status of the payments of the taxes

- The period each payment covers.

In some parts of the country, it is customary for property owners to receive and pay two sets of real estate taxes per year.

Regardless of the number of times payments are required, the method of prorating the tax payments will be the same. The only change that will occur will be that the final tax figures will be based on two separate sets of calculations.

To prorate taxes, you must first determine the due date of each tax payment.

- We will assume that the tax-billing period is due April 1.

You will next determine the period this billing covers.

- We will assume that the tax-billing due on April 1 is for the period of January though December 31.

The status of the payment dictates whether the seller receives tax payment reimbursement from the buyer or if the seller is required to remit tax funds for the payment of the tax billing at the time of closing.

- We will assume the tax payment was made as required by the seller on or before the due date.

Using a closing date of May 20 and the assumptions, you would perform the calculations to determine the monthly and daily tax rate by taking the total of the yearly taxes. In our example the

- > :Yearly Taxes total $585.00. You will divide this total figure by 12 months to determine the monthly tax costs of the property. In our example that total is $48.75 per month

  $585.00   /   12   = $48.75 per month

- > We have determined that the Monthly Taxes equal $48.75. Since we are using a 30-day month, we will divide the monthly figure by 30 to determine that the daily tax rate equals $1.625.

  $ 48.75   /   30   = $ 1.625 daily rate

- > The Seller Portion of the taxes covers the period of January 1 though May   20.

  You will take the $48.75 monthly figure and multiply it by the four months allocated to the seller to total $195.00.

  $48.75   x   4   = $195.00

  You will then take the $1.625 daily figure and multiply it by the 20 extra days allocated to the seller to total $32.50.

  $ 1.625   x   20   = $ 32.50

  You will add the total of the monthly calculations and the daily calculations to determine that the total taxes assessed to the seller equals $227.50.

$195.00 + 32.50 = $227.50

> This example leaves the Buyers Portion of the taxes to cover the period of May 21 through December 31.

You have the baseline figures for both the monthly and daily tax rate from your seller allocation calculations.

You will use again use the $48.75 monthly figure but this time you multiply it by the 7 months allocated to the buyer. The monthly total allocated to the buyer equals 341.25.

$48.75 x 7 = $341.25

You will then take the daily figure of 1.625 and multiply it by the 10 days remaining in the month. 10 days plus the 20 days already accounted for on the sellers side equals the 30-day month. This calculation example has the buyer paying $16.25 to cover the daily allocation of the taxes.

$ 1.625 x 10 = $ 16.25

You will then add the $341.25 monthly figure to the $16.25 daily figure to determine that the total taxes assessed to the buyer equals $357.50.

$341.25 + $16.25 = $357.50

> You may confirm that your calculations are correct by adding the buyer portion and the seller portion and then comparing it to the total taxes due on the property.

If the tax payments are due twice yearly, you will calculate the second payment in the same manner and add both figures to achieve a total allocation of the taxes.

The figures will be entered as either a positive or a negative on the good faith estimate depending on the status of the payment.

> In other words, payment for the taxes due has been made by the seller, the borrower will repay the seller for their portion at the settlement table.

> If taxes due have not been paid by the seller, the sellers tax portion will be given back to the borrower as part of the settlement process.

This figure can be entered as a positive figure on the good faith estimate.

The ability to enter a positive in this column may make a difference to the ability to close the transaction if the borrower is extremely cash poor.

HAZARD INSURANCE

Hazard insurance is typically paid in advance based on the billing received from the hazard insurance company providing the coverage. At the beginning of each year of the policy, the premium for that year's coverage must be paid. At times, a billing cycle such as monthly or quarterly payments may be negotiated with the insurance company. When real estate is sold, the borrower may ask the seller to transfer the current insurance coverage or may obtain new coverage through the insurance company of their choice. If the existing coverage is transferred, the premiums required will be allocated to the borrower and seller respectively based upon the date of the closing or other date as negotiated in the sales contract.

You will need to obtain information pertaining to the insurance coverage to begin the process of prorating the premiums. This might include

- The frequency of payment for the policy

- The total premium of the policy

- The exact term covered by the policy premium

  Example: A payment is made one time of year.

  The total premium is $660 per coverage period.

  The coverage period extends from November 1 to October 31.

  The sales contract negotiates that:

  - the borrower will assume the sellers insurance policy from the date of closing

  - closing is held on May 1

  Both the buyer and the seller will be responsible for 50% of the total premium.

  The seller has paid the premium in full in advance

  The buyer owes the seller exactly $330 for the insurance Coverage

Closings dates typically do not occur on a neat, evenly divided basis. Therefore, the pro-rata calculations will often require more in-depth calculations than described in the above example. It is typically necessary to divide the premium coverage year into months and then divide the months into days to complete the calculations.

Using the previous example, suppose the closing occurred on April 30 instead of May 1. This would give the buyer 6 months and 1 day of coverage.

The first step in calculating the exact figure the borrower owes the seller is to divide the total premium into 12 monthly premium figures.

$660 premium   /   by 12 months   = $55.00 per month

The next step is to divide the monthly premium into a daily cost basis.

$55.00 monthly figure /   30 days in a month   = $1.8333 per day

Next, you will multiply the monthly rate by the term the buyer will obtain

6 months   x $55.00 monthly figure = $330.00

Next, you will multiply the daily rate by the daily term the buyer will obtain

1 day   x   the daily figure $1.8333 = $ 1.83

The Total buyer premium is $331.83

All figures will be rounded up or down to achieve a final figure to the nearest 1 cent.

Truth-In-Lending Act Regulation Z

The Truth-in-Lending act is a part of the Consumer Credit Protection Act. The Truth-in-Lending act is meant to protect and inform the consumer by requiring disclosures regarding loan terms and costs. This regulation applies to all institutions offering credit to a consumer.

- The Truth-in-Lending act allows the borrower to compare the cost of a cash transaction against the costs of a credit transaction.

- The Truth-in-Lending act also provides an easy to understand format for borrowers when comparing one lending institutions terms against those of another lending institution.

The regulations require lenders to:

- Disclose the maximum, potential interest rate for all variable rate transactions.

- Limit home equity plans that incorporate the costs of financing in the principal balance of the loan.

- Adhere to disclosure standards for advertisement that refer to credit terms.

- Provide borrowers with fair rights of rescission.

You should provide your borrower with specific disclosures to comply with Regulation Z. These include:

- Arm Loan disclosure.

- Right of rescission notice

- Advertising practice disclosures

The Truth-in-Lending act also requires that lenders make certain disclosures concerning THE REAL ESTATE SETTLEMENT PROCEDURES ACT. These disclosures must be provided with in three days of an application for credit. The initial disclosures will be partially based upon information provided by the borrower. A final series of disclosures will be provided at the time of settlement that contains the confirmed and final information regarding the loan and loan terms.

It is important that you understand the

DEFINITION OF TRUTH-IN-LENDING TERMS

The **Annual Percentage Rate** is not the Note rate or the quoted interest rate for which the borrower applied. The Annual Percentage Rate is the cost of the loan in percentage terms. The Annual Percentage Rate takes into account a variety of loan charges; interest is only one of these charges. Other charges that are used in the calculation of the Annual Percentage Rate are Private mortgage insurance costs (when applicable) and any Prepaid Finance Charges including loan discount, origination fees, prepaid interest and any other credit costs added to the loan package. The Annual Percentage Rate is calculated by spreading the cost of these charges over the life of the loan, which results in a higher rate than the interest rate shown on the Mortgage. If interest were the only Finance Charge, the interest rate and the Annual Percentage Rate would be the same. When creating the Good Faith Estimate, it is important to consider charges that will affect the Annual Percentage Rate.

Prepaid Finance Charges are charges made in connection with the loan that must be paid at the closing of the loan. The Federal Reserve Board Regulation Z defines these charges. The borrower must pay these charges. Some examples of the charges are Origination Fee, Discount Fee, PMI, and Tax Service Fee. Some loan charges such as appraisal fees and credit report fees are excluded from the Prepaid Finance Charges.

The **Finance Charge** is the amount of interest, prepaid finance charges and certain insurance premiums that the borrower is expected to pay over the life of the loan.

The **Amount Financed** is the loan amount the borrower is obtaining less any prepaid finance charges. The Prepaid Finance Charges are found on the Good Faith Estimate. For example, if the borrowers note is for $100,000 and the prepaid finance charges are $5,000 then the amount financed is equal to $95,000. The Amount Financed is the amount on which the Annual Percentage Rate is based.

The **Total of Payments** figure represents the total of all of the payments that will be made toward principal, interest, and mortgage insurance over the life of the loan.

The figure represented in the **Payment Schedule** represents principal, interest, plus private mortgage insurance payments that will be made over the life of the loan. These figures do not reflect taxes and insurance escrows or any buy down payments that were contributed by the seller.

2:23 TIL Definitions

Adjustable Rate Mortgage Disclosure

If a borrower's primary dwelling is going to be secured by an Adjustable Rate or Variable Rate loan, The Truth-in-Lending act requires that additional disclosures be provided, with regard to the Adjustable Rate Mortgage.

An adjustable rate mortgage is a mortgage program that carries a variable interest rate that can change over the life of the loan. The rate of an adjustable rate mortgage may go up or down depending on the status of the index to which it is linked.

Adjustable-rate mortgage programs are created with a pre-set margin with the margin base set on a major mortgage index such as the Libor. An adjustable rate mortgage program has the ability to affect the borrower's monthly payments through the application of the new interest rate occurring at each adjustment period. This adjusted rate could place some borrowers at risk if economic conditions dictate that the rate goes up and the borrower's debt to income ratio is unable to bear the payment applied because of the increased interest rate.

When working with a borrower that is obtaining an adjustable rate mortgage, you must provide the borrower with educational notices and disclosures that assist them in understanding the loan program that they are obtaining.

- The Consumer Handbook on Adjustable Rate Mortgages

- A disclosure for each variable rate program offered to the borrower.

The disclosures must contain all the necessary information required by Regulation Z.

The Truth-in-Lending Act also requires loan services to provide disclosures to consumers each month an adjustment to the interest rate occurs.

ADJUSTABLE RATE MORTGAGE DISCLOSURE STATEMENT

IMPORTANT MORTGAGE LOAN INFORMATION - PLEASE READ CAREFULLY

PROGRAM NAME: _____

You have expressed an interest in applying for an Adjustable Rate Mortgage loan (ARM). This disclosure contains information regarding the differences between this ARM and other mortgage loans. This disclosure describes the features of the specific ARM that you are considering. Upon request, we will provide you with information about any other Adjustable Rate Mortgage programs we have available.

ADJUSTABLE RATE MORTGAGE LOAN: This loan is an Adjustable Rate Mortgage loan. The interest rate may change based upon movements of a specific interest rate index. Changes in the interest rate will be reflected by increases or decreases for payments. The date or dates on which changes can occur will be specified in the ARM loan documents. This ARM is based on the terms and conditions of the program in which you have expressed an interest. We have based this disclosure on recent interest rates, index and margin values, and fees.

THIS DISCLOSURE: This disclosure is not a contract or loan commitment. The matters discussed in this disclosure are subject to change by us at any time without notice. DETERMINING THE INTEREST RATE: Your interest rate will be determined by means of an index that is subject to change.

Your interest rate is based on the Index value plus a margin. A change in the index generally will result in a change in the interest rate. If the Index rate change since the previous adjustment is less than _____, the interest rate will not change. The amount that your interest rate change may also be affected by periodic interest rate change limitations and the lifetime interest rate limits set forth in your loan program.

    Interest Rate Adjustments Your interest rate under this ARM can change every _____ years.

    Your interest rate cannot increase or decrease more than ____ percentage points at each adjustment.

    Your interest rate cannot increase or decrease more than ____percentage points over the term of your loan.

    Rate adjustments under this ARM will be reflected in higher or lower payments.

DETERMINING THE PAYMENTS: Your initial monthly payment of principal and interest will be determined based on the interest rate, loan term, and loan balance when your loan is closed. Your payment will be set to amortize the loan over a period of ___ payments.

Frequency of Payment Changes: Based on increases or decreases in the Index, payment amounts under this ARM loan can change every ____ years. Your monthly payment amount could change more frequently if there is a change in other loan factors not relating to the ARM. These factors may include taxes, assessments, insurance premiums, or other charges required when creating an escrow or impound account.

Limitations on Payment Changes: Your payment can change every ___ years based on changes in the interest rate, loan term, or loan balance.

Adjustment Notices: You will be notified if interest rate changes occur. If an interest rate change effects your monthly payment, you will be notified at least 25 calendar days before the changed payment is due. The notice will indicate the adjusted payment amount, interest rate, Index value, and the outstanding loan balance at that time.

** INSERT AN EXAMPLE AND INDEX TABLES AS THEY APPLY TO THE ARM UNDER DISCUSSION.

I/we acknowledge that we have received a copy of this disclosure:

Borrower Signature   Date   Co-Borrower Signature   Date

2:24 Sample Form –ARM Disclosure – HUD Release

Homeownership Equity Protection Act (HOEPA)

The Homeownership Equity Protection Act of 1994 is designed to protect the borrower against unfair and abusive lending tactics. This act was created as an amendment to the Truth-in- Lending Act Regulation Z.

The Homeownership Equity Protection Act establishes requirements regarding interest rates and fees. The loans covered under the Homeownership Equity Protection Act include

- First mortgage transactions where the Annual Percentage Rate exceeds 8% of the current prime rate as established by the Treasury securities of comparable maturity

- Second mortgage transactions in which the Annual Percentage Rate exceeds 10% of the current prime rate as established by the Treasury securities index of comparable maturity.

- Loans where the total fees and points paid by the borrower exceed 8% of the total loan amount or the fixed figure established yearly. The greater of the two costs is used to establish requirements.

The loans affected by this act are generally termed high-rate or high-fee loans. This type of loan is seen more frequently within the sub-prime industry than the prime industry.

The Act does not include provisions regarding construction loans, reverse mortgage transactions, or equity lines of credit.

You must provide specific disclosures to the borrower regarding the loan terms and fees:

- Right to cancel

- Specific information regarding Annual Percentage Rate, monthly payment amounts, and the loan amount

- Variable rate or Adjustable rate mortgages require an additional disclosure that states the monthly payment and the interest rate are subject to change. The disclosure must state the maximum amount of change that may occur.

Homeowners Protection Act of 1998

In 1998, additional homeowner protection regulations were put into place. These regulations are designed to assist the borrower in understanding and minimizing the private mortgage insurance costs accrued.

Private mortgage insurance is used to allow more individuals to purchase homes with a minimal amount of cash down payment. Private mortgage insurance is required by most lenders until the borrower obtains an equity position in the home of greater than 20%.

> Private mortgage insurance benefits the borrower in that the placement of the insurance enables the borrower to obtain home financing without a large cash down payment.

> Private mortgage insurance requirements can be removed if the borrower is able to pay 20% of the sales price in down payment.

Since some borrowers are unable to provide 20% of the sales price in cash at the time of closing, purchasing the Private mortgage insurance policy enables the lender to provide financing while minimizing risk.

Once a borrower reaches an equity position of 20% of the property value Private mortgage insurance, premiums are no longer needed to protect the position of the lender. At this point borrowers are no longer required to continue making yearly premium payments. Processes have been put into place to enable the borrower to cancel the Private mortgage insurance policy when the required equity position in the property has been reached.

Borrower Initiated Cancellation

The Homeowner Protection Act of 1998 provides remedies for cancellation of the Private mortgage insurance coverage and an end to the yearly premium payments. A homeowner who has a 20% equity position in the property and a good payment history on their loan may request that their Private mortgage insurance be cancelled.

A borrower may initiate a cancellation request if:

- The loan has reached an 80% LTV based upon the initial amortization schedule provided to the borrower. Adjustable rate mortgages are based on Adjustable Amortization Schedules.

- The borrower has a good payment history.

  A good payment history dictates that No mortgage payments were made more than 60 days late with in the preceding 24-month period.

The borrower must be able to illustrate that no mortgage payments were made more than 30 days late within the proceeding 12-month period

- The mortgage holder must approve the valuation of the property through verified methods such as the appraised value.

- The equity position must be free and clear.

No subordinate liens may be held against the equity position of 20%.

Automatic Cancellation

The borrower is not required to take action to cancel the policy. Under the act, the policy will be subject to Automatic Cancellation.

- The Homeowner Protection Act requires that the Private Mortgage Insurance be automatically cancelled when the borrower's equity position reaches 22%.

- When a mortgage, which is subject to Private Mortgage Insurance reaches a 78% Loan to value, based upon the initial amortization schedule, the Private Mortgage Insurance must be automatically terminated if the borrower is current on mortgage payment obligations.

- If the borrower is not current on mortgage payment obligations, the Private Mortgage Insurance must be terminated when the borrower brings their balance current.

High-Risk Mortgages

Certain high-risk mortgages may be subject to an alteration in the rules of cancellation for private mortgage insurance policies.

The Homeowner Protection Act bases the determination of a high-risk loan on the guidelines defined by Fannie Mae and Freddie Mac. The Private Mortgage Insurance payments on a high-risk loan are automatically terminated when the loan reaches a 77% loan to value or the term reaches half-life. The cancellation is based upon whichever level occurs first.

PRIVATE MORTGAGE INSURANCE INITIAL DISCLOSURE

Borrower:_____ Co-Borrower:_____

Property Address:_____

PRIVATE MORTGAGE INSURANCE TERMINATION DISCLOSURE

We <u>SAMPLE MORTGAGE COMPANY</u> require that you <u>BORROWER NAME</u> maintain private mortgage insurance ("PMI") in connection with your mortgage loan. PMI protects lenders and others against financial loss in case of borrower default. Federal law provides you with the right to cancel PMI under certain circumstances. Federal law establishes when PMI must be terminated. This Disclosure describes those cancellation and termination rights.

___1.   We have provided you with an initial amortization schedule. Federal Law basis the cancellation and termination terms on this initial amortization schedule.

___2. Borrower Initiated Cancellation: A borrower may initiate cancellation if certain requirements are satisfied.

   Term Requirements of Cancellation:

   You have the right to request cancellation of PMI at any time on or after:

   The date that the principal balance of the loan, based on the initial amortization schedule, reaches 80% of the original value (lesser of sales price or appraised value) of the property securing the loan.

   The date that the principal balance of the loan, based on actual payments made, reaches 80% of the original value (lesser of the sales price or appraised value) of the property securing the loan.

   Status Requirements for Cancellation:

   PMI may be cancelled when you reach the stated percentage if you meet all of the following requirements:

   You must submit your cancellation request in writing to the servicer of your loan.

   You must have a good payment history on your loan.

   A good payment history is described as a history where you have not made a mortgage payment that was 60 days or longer past due during the 24 months preceding the cancellation date.

   The description of a good payment history also requires you have not made a mortgage payment that was 30 days or longer past due during the 12 months proceeding the cancellation date.

   You must have provided the note holder with

   Evidence that the value of the property securing the not has not declined below its original value

   Certification that you do not have a subordinate lien on the equity in the property

___3.   Automatic Termination: If mortgage loan payments are current, PMI will automatically terminate when the principal balance of the loan is scheduled to reach 78% of the original value (lesser of sales price or appraised value) of the property based on the initial amortization schedule.

   The loan servicer will notify you when the automatic cancellation of PMI occurs.

___4.   Exemptions

There are certain exemptions to the right to cancellation and automatic termination of PMI. These exemptions relate to certain mortgage loans with higher risks associated with the extension of credit. These exemptions do not apply to your loan transaction.

I/We have received a copy of this Private Mortgage Insurance Termination Disclosure.

Borrower Signature   Date   Co-Borrower Signature   Date

2:25 Sample Form – Private Mortgage Insurance Initial Disclosure – HUD Release

PMI Disclosure Requirements

Loans that carry Private Mortgage Insurance have additional Disclosure Requirements.

If you conduct a transaction that is subject to Private Mortgage Insurance, you must provide certain specific disclosures to the borrower in relationship to the transaction.

- A written initial amortization schedule based on loan terms at the time of the loan

- The date the borrower may cancel based on the Initial Amortization Schedule only.

- Notice that the borrower may request cancellation in accordance with the requirements set forth in the borrower cancellation portion of the Act.

- Notice that Automatic Cancellation will occur at the termination date as defined by the Initial Amortization Schedule.

- Notice concerning exemptions to the cancellation pertaining to High-Risk loans

Flood Disaster Protection Act of 1973

Because of increased losses to homeowners from floods and mudslides, the Flood Disaster Protection Act implemented a National Flood Insurance Program that increased limits of insurance coverage and the amount of insurance outstanding in flood prone communities.

The need for a revision of the flood insurance system was determined because of population growth and the need to establish community centers in areas of the country with a higher flood potential.

- The Act increased the limits of coverage under the National Flood Insurance Program.

- The Act provides for identification concerning flood prone areas.

- The Act requires State and Local communities to participate in flood insurance programs and to adopt flood plain ordinances.

- The Act requires the purchase of flood insurance by property owners who own or acquire land located in areas identified as having special flood hazards.

Each borrower must fully understand his rights and obligations under the Flood Disaster Protection Act.

NOTICE OF SPECIAL FLOOD HAZARDS
NOTICE OF AVAILABILITY OF FEDERAL DISASTER RELIEF ASSISTANCE

The property securing the loan for which you have applied is located in an area identified as having special flood hazards.

The area is identified by FEMA as a special flood hazard area using FEMA's Flood Insurance Rate Map or the Flood Hazard Boundary Map for the following community:

This area has at least a one- percent chance of a flood equal to or exceeding the base flood elevation or 100-year flood plain in any given year. During the live of a 30-year mortgage loan, the risk of a 100-year flood in a special, flood hazard area is twenty-six percent.

Federal law allows the lender and the borrower to request the Director of FEMA to review the determination of the location as a special, flood hazard area. If you would like to make such a request please contact our offices at

The community in which the property is located participates in the National Flood Insurance Program (NFIP). Federal law does not allow us to make the loan you have applied for if you do not purchase flood insurance. The flood insurance purchased must be maintained for the life of the loan. If you fail to purchase or renew the flood insurance on the property, Federal Law authorizes and requires us to purchase the flood insurance for you at your expense.

Flood insurance must cover the lesser of

   The outstanding principal balance of the loan

   The maximum amount of coverage allowed for this type of property under NFIP.

Federal disaster-relief assistance may be available for damages incurred in excess of your flood insurance coverage. TO qualify for Federal Disaster Relief, your community must participate in the NFIP in accordance with NFIP requirements.

Borrower(s) agree to furnish at the borrower(s) expense, a flood insurance policy that meets the lender's requirements on or before closing of the loan.

2:26 Sample Form – Notice of Special Flood Hazards – Notice of Availability of Federal Disaster Relief Assistance – HUD Release

Chapter 3

BORROWER PRE-QUALIFICATION

From the moment you first speak with a prospective borrower, you should be gathering information and planning how you will process the loan. Many Loan Processors fail to achieve their goals for the simple reason that they are afraid to ask for information.

Information is your most valuable tool in planning a loan processing strategy. Obtaining information is quite simple if you just get over the natural shyness of asking strangers for personal information. You will find that, as a professional, people will answer almost any question you ask. However, you must ask!

On the next page, you will find a "Pre-approval Questionnaire" that we recommend using for each prospective borrower. Most of your initial contacts will be over the telephone. If you have this form handy, preferably bound in a notebook, you will always be able to lead the conversation exactly where you, as the loan processor, need it to go.

The pre-approval questionnaire is your most important ally. Most of the information required when pre-certifying a loan package is included in the questionnaire. In fact, much of the basic information that will be required for the residential mortgage application is included. This allows you to pre-fill some information, subject to verification during the application interview. Pre-filling saves time and allows you and the borrower to focus on the loan process requirements.

Pre-Qualification Questionnaire Date: _____

Referral: _____ Phone: _____

Borrower Name: _____ Co-Borrower Name: _____

Home Phone: _____ Other Phone: _____ Best time(s) to call: _____

DOB: _____ SSN: _____ DOB: _____ SSN: _____

May I run a credit report?___ Yes ___ No   May I run a credit report? ___ Yes ___ No

Employer: _____ Employer: _____

Address: _____ Address: _____

Phone: _____ No yrs. ___ Position: _____ Phone: _____ No yrs. ___ Position: _____

Current Address: _____ Check? ___ Yes ___ No

Landlord/Mortgage Holder: _____ Phone: _____

Rent _____ Own ___ No. Yrs: ___ Have you chosen a home to purchase? ___ Yes ___ No Value$_____

___ 1st ___2nd ___Rate/Term Refi ___ C/O Refi ___ Special: _____

Gross Income		Debt	
Borrowers Mthly	$_____	Mortgage/Rental Payment	$_____
Prev Year	$_____	Auto Payment	$_____
Co-Borrowers Mthly	$_____	Auto Payment #2	$_____
Prev Year	$_____	Installment Debt / Type _____	$_____
Other Income _____	$_____	Installment Debt / Type _____	$_____
Other Income _____	$_____	Other _____	$_____
Total Income	$_____	Total Debt	$_____

DTI _____%

Explanation of Credit Situation/Notes: _____

_____

_____

_____

Outcome:

Taken By: _____

L/P: _____

Pre-qualification Questionnaire Key

Date

You will always want to date the query.

You may need to 'shelve' a query until an issue has seasoned.

It is our recommendation that you bind each month's questionnaires in a master folder for tracking of referral sources, inquiries vs. applications and other numbers that will affect your career.

You will want to keep a copy of any query that does not lead to a full application for follow-up marketing.

Referral

You will want to have referral information available so you may provide follow-up information.

Tracking referral source information will allow you to assess your branches marketing and advertising effort effectiveness.

Telephone Number

You will want to have the referral partner's telephone number handy to assist you in maintaining communication.

Look these up yourself, DO **NOT** require your borrower to find the number for you.

Keeping referral partners informed of the progress of a package is one of your greatest assets.

These updates provide a fabulous reason for a face-to-face 'call' on a referral partner and their office.

Referral partners appreciate frequent updates. Referral partners are reluctant to work with a loan processor who does not consistently provide status information concerning the status of a borrower's application.

Borrower Name

You will need the full name including middle initial and any additional information Jr., Sr., II

Do not use nicknames.

Note any aliases that the borrower commonly uses.

Names, especially among family, can be very similar.

The more identifying information you can acquire the more pure your credit report will be.

Co-Borrower Name

Some applications will not have a co-borrower.

When a co-borrower exists, it is important to acquire correct identifying information for this person to ensure sufficient pre-qualification data is available.

If the co-borrower information is not readily available at the time of the call, complete the primary borrower information and request the applicant telephone you later the same day with the co-borrower information.

Date of Birth/Social Security Number etc

This information is important for the loan application and vital when you are pulling a credit report.

Always pull credit reports separately.

Even if the borrower and co-borrower are married, you will want to have separate reports.

There are times you will want to drop one borrower in an effort to improve loan grades.

May I run a credit report?

It is imperative that you obtain permission to pull a borrower's credit report.

You will have the borrower sign the credit consent forms later in the loan process.

Consent must be available before you may run the report.

You may not run a credit report on any individual without their consent.

Employer

This information aids you in determining some of the issues that may arise during the course of the loan.

If there is a history of job changes or there is not a 2-year employment history a problem may exist during documentation. Issues such as these are red flags.

Number of years at present employment

You are looking for a minimum of two years employment history.

If the borrower/co-borrower has not been in their current employment two years, you will need to trace back under comments until you acquire a complete two-year history.

This is an excellent reference when you have an application that requires an exception. A common compensating factor is 'at current employment more than 5 years'.

Current Address

This is identifying information you will want to have to clarify identity on the credit report.

Do you rent or own?

This allows you to determine potential source of funds, loan product possibilities and additional documentation that you may require from the borrower.

Landlord/Mortgage Holder

It is important to determine from the start if the borrower pays an entity or an individual for their housing expense.

You can verify payments to an entity via VOR/VOM but an individual will typically require checks for verification of payment history.

Do you pay by check?

This question is important if the borrower or co-borrower rents or is purchasing from an individual.

If your borrower or co-borrower rents or is buying from an individual and does not pay by check, you will typically need to acquire alternate documentation as proof of rental/mortgage payment history.

Number of years at Present address?

You will need a two-year residence history for each borrower on the application.

If the borrower has been at the current residence less than two years, you will need to add in comments any additional residence history until you obtain two full years.

This is an excellent reference when you have an application that requires an exception. A common compensating factor is 'at current residence more than 5 years'.

Have you chosen a home to purchase?

You will want to determine the urgency of the query and if the borrower is currently working with an Agent.

If no Agent is working with the borrower, you will want to take the opportunity to refer the borrower to an affinity member with whom you would like to establish a referral relationship.

Perform all referrals after you have the borrower commitment to your programs. Since you do not have a referring relationship built with the referral partner, they may refer these borrowers to another lender if you do not obtain the commitment before sending the borrower to the partner.

Value

This question pertains to the package even if they have not chosen a home to purchase.

You will want to get an idea of their expectations and the price range they are considering.

The loan officer will need to take this figure and determine if their expectations are reasonable and fit into their DTI.

Often borrowers are very high or very low in their estimate of what they are able to afford.

The loan officer will want to pre-qualify the borrower for the highest amount they feel comfortably fits their budget.

Type of Loan

1st Mortgage, 2nd Mortgage, Rate or Term Refinance, Cash-out Refinance.

Knowing the type of loan the borrower or co-borrower believes they desire, allows the loan officer to begin planning the loan structure and matrix placement from the moment of query.

You will find some product approvals vary greatly depending on the type of loan.

Income Information

In order to pre-qualify a package you must have complete income information.

Many loan denials occur due to excessive DTI Ratios.

All income should be entered even if the borrower does not wish to use all income as qualifying income or if not all the income can be used as qualifying income. This is an excellent reference when you have an application that requires an exception. Income is a part of many compensating factors.

Debt Information

Debt load will be visible on the Credit Report but it is important to ask a borrower this information. There may be new debt, which is not yet showing on the report but may crop up before closing the loan.

Child support and alimony payments do affect the debt load.

Explanation of credit situation?

This is the opportunity for notes.

Your borrowers will usually explain any information that is present on their credit report.

Gathering this information now allows you to pre-plan the loan package, request any additional documentation that you may need and is an excellent reference if problems appear later in the loan process.

Outcome

You will want to note what happened with the query.

Some queries will lead to an application.

You will file other queries for follow-up when an issue is resolved.

Keeping a file of this information allows you to track your numbers in future months.

Outcome is important if the borrower's are working with an agent.

You will want immediate documentation if the package dies at query so your agent is not spending valuable time working with borrower's who you cannot qualify at this time.

Lending is a service business. The final analysis shows that our most important "product" is our professionalism, attentiveness, and responsiveness to our borrowers. Much of our communication is on the telephone.

Whether you are communicating with a borrower, prospect, or others on the telephone or in person, the impression that you convey creates an image in the person's mind. This image will affect your future relationship with that person. For those reasons, it is important that your conversations are controlled and concise. A complete course on telephone and conversational control is available in our advanced program offerings. For now, you must focus on learning career basics. To assist you we have provided a script to allow you to flow smoothly through the pre-qualification process.

The pre-approval questionnaire offers an excellent tool for structuring your first contact.

The proper way to use the questionnaire is as follows:

L/P: Good morning/afternoon/evening, <u>Your Company Name</u> this is <u>Your Name</u>, may I help you?

Borrower: They will state the reason for there call and very likely explain their situation.

L/P: Do you have a few minutes to answer a couple of questions?

Borrower: Since they made the call to you, they will typically have a few minutes to spare while they determine if you have a program to fit their situation.

L/P: Could you tell me how you were referred to us? (DO NOT ask for details such as telephone number of referral source – you can look this information up yourself).

L/P: What is your name?

L/P: Will you be on loan alone or with someone else? (Keep in mind that it is occasionally prudent to cut either the borrower or co-borrower from the loan later in the process. This is a decision will be made based on credit scores and/or income and debt ratios.

L/P: What is your Date of Birth?

L/P: What is your Social Security Number?

L/P: May I run a credit report?

You are looking for a yes. None of the other information you acquire will aid you in any way if you cannot see what type of credit situation you are dealing with. The approval to run a credit report signifies a commitment on the part of the borrower to your loan program.

L/P: Where are you employed?

L/P: How long have you been there?

If they have been at their current employment less than two years, you will need to acquire two full years' employment history before completing the application.

L/P: What is your position?

L/P: Ask for the same information for the co-borrower.

L/P: What is your current address?

L/P: How long have you lived there?

L/P: Do you rent or own the home?

L/P: Who is your landlord or mortgage holder?

If the landlord or lender is a company there is no need for further documentation, it will typically appear on the credit report. However, if the landlord/mortgage holder is an individual, more documentation will be required to prove a mortgage/rental history.

L/P: Do you pay by cash or check?

This question only applies in the event that their landlord/mortgage holder is an individual.

L/P: Have you chosen a home to purchase?

This will allow you to rate the urgency of the file. A borrower who has not begun the home search process will be less urgent than a borrower with a sales contract in hand.

L/P: Do you know the amount you are looking to spend?

This question allows the loan officer to determine from the start if their spending expectations are set too high for some of the loan products and place them accordingly.

L/P: What is your monthly income?

You will frequently need to do the math yourself. Accept the income they give you whether they provide yearly, monthly, or weekly income figures.

L/P: Do you have income you wish use from any other source: rental property, alimony, child support etc?

A borrower is not required to use additional income as part of the approval criteria. If the borrower wishes to use other income, it is allowable.

L/P: Obtain the same information for the co-borrower.

L/P: What is your monthly rent/mortgage payment?

L/P: What is your car payment?

L/P: Do you have a second car?

L/P: Do you have any credit cards or personal loans?

L/P   What are the monthly payments?

                A borrower's debt load will be visible on the credit report but it is advisable to review the debts with the borrower to limit surprises later in the process.

Throughout the questionnaire, the borrower will be giving you information that you will want to note in the explanation of credit situation section. This aids you in determining the special circumstances surrounding this loan package.

Upon completion of the questionnaire, you will want to assure the borrower that they ARE your borrower, plan to pre-qualify their questionnaire and set an appointment to meet face-to-face, verify their information, and discuss their loan options. A sample of how to do this smoothly is as follows:

L/P: Ok, I plan to pass this information over to _____. They will be working with us to during the early stages of your loan. We will review your information tonight to see what programs will work best for your situation. Are you available <u>date not more than two days away</u>?

Borrower: Answers positive or negative

L/P: Set up an appointment.

L/P: Ok, when you come I will need you to bring a few things. I will need (below are the most common items to request – you will need to refer to documenting a loan package for detailed information):

                W-2's from the last two years

                Proof of any additional income you want me to consider – child support order, divorce decree

                Any proof you have concerning (whatever their special credit situation BK, Divorce Decree, etc.)

                12 months cancelled rent checks (if paying an individual)

L/P: Ok then, I will see you on <u>date</u> at <u>time</u> if there are any problems, please give me a call.

Upon completion of the questionnaire, you will be able to pre-qualify a borrower. Providing you obtained their permission, your next step is to pull a credit report and provide the entire pre-qualification package to the loan officer so they may determine initial purchase levels and possible loan programs.

Chapter 4

THE SALES AGREEMENT

A sales agreement that is correctly prepared and endorsed is a binding contract that holds each applicable party responsible for the terms negotiated within the contract. Once the sales agreement is written and signed, all of the parties are obligated to complete the transaction providing the terms of the contract can be legally met. An essential element of the sales contract and one of the reasons that a sales agreement may become null and void are the clauses relevant to the mortgage-financing portion of the transaction.

The sales agreement will dictate the handling of many matters with regard to both the pre-close activities that you must facilitate to ensure a timely closing and the type and terms of the mortgage loan that are acceptable under the contract. It is critical that you become familiar with all entries on a real estate sales contract and the proper action dictated by each item included within the contract.

A sales agreement may take many forms and include all of the entries on the example included for your review, additional entries created by the parties involved in the transaction or just some of the entries. If a sales agreement is privately created between the buyer and the seller, some information essential to the loan process may not be included. It is up to you to confirm that all of the required details are included in the sales contract or to gain the necessary information from the buyer and the seller prior to proceeding with the loan structure, order of affinity services, or closing processes.

This segment will assist you in understanding the clauses with the standard real estate sales contract that are most critical to the process from your perspective. Additional sections and clauses are included for your review. You should gain a basic familiarity with all areas of a standard residential sales agreement and focus more intensely on those sections that apply directly to the mortgage finance details of the transaction.

It is important to remember that a sales agreement may take many forms and that addenda can be created to the sales agreement. Addenda will typically address items of specific importance to the parties involved and will often create additional requirements or negotiations that will bind the parties. These clauses, requirements, and negotiation elements will alter the handling of the transaction and should be reviewed with care. Any alteration to the sales agreement should be scrutinized to ensure that the applicable party completes each action required of the transaction according to the expectations of the involved parties.

STANDARD AGREEMENT FOR THE SALE OF REAL ESTATE

SELLERS BUISNES RELATIONSHIP WITH LICENSED BROKER
Broker (company) _____ Phone _____
Address _____ Fax _____
Licensee(s) _____ Designated Agent __ Yes __ No
BROKER IS THE AGNET FOR THE SELLER   OR (if checked below):
Broker is NOT the Agent for the seller and is a/an: __ AGENT FOR BUYER __ Transaction Licensee

BUYERS BUISNES RELATIONSHIP WITH LICENSED BROKER
Broker (company) _____ Phone _____
Address _____ Fax _____
Licensee(s) _____ Designated Agent __ Yes __ No
BROKER IS THE AGNET FOR THE BUYER   OR (if checked below):
Broker is NOT the Agent for the seller and is a/an: __ AGENT FOR SELLER __ Transaction Licensee

When the same Broker is Agent for Buyer, Broker is a Dual Agent. All of Broker's licensees are also Dual Agents UNLESS there is a separate Designated Agents for Buyer and Seller. If the same Licensee is designated for Seller and Buyer, the Licensee is a Dual Agent.

1. *This Agreement*, dated _____ is between SELLER(S):
_____, called Seller, and
BUYER(S): _____ , called Buyer.

2. PROPERTY Seller herby agrees to sell and convey to Buyer, who hereby agrees to purchase:
ALL THAT CERTAIN lot or piece of ground with buildings and improvements thereon erected, if any, known as:
_____
_____
In the _____ of _____ County of _____ in the State of
_____. Identification (e.g., Tax ID#, Parcel #; Lot, Block; Deed Book, Page,
Recording Date): _____

3. TERMS
(A) Purchase Price _____
_____ U.S. Dollars
which will be paid to the Seller by the Buyer as follows:
  1. Cash or check at the signing of this Agreement_____ $ _____
  2. Cash or check within ____ days of the execution of this agreement_____ $ _____
  3. _____ _____ $ _____
  4. Cash or cashiers check at the time of settlement_____ $ _____
                              TOTAL $ _____

(B) Deposits paid by Buyer within ____ DAYS of settlement will be by cash or cashiers check. Deposits, regardless of the form of payment and the person designated as payee, will be paid in U.S. Dollars to Broker for Seller (unless otherwise stated here) _____
_____ who will retain deposits in an escrow account until consummation or termination of this Agreement in conformity with all applicable laws and regulations. Any check tendered as deposit monies may be held uncashed pending the acceptance of this agreement.
(C) Seller's written approval to be on or before _____
(D) Settlement to be on _____ or before if Buyer and Seller agree
(E) Settlement will occur in the county where the Property is located or in an adjacent county, during normal business hours, unless Buyer and Seller agree otherwise.
(F) Conveyance from Seller will be by fee simple deed of Special Warranty unless otherwise stated here _____
_____
(G) Payment of transfer taxes will be divided equally between Buyer and Seller unless otherwise stated here _____
_____
(H) At the time of settlement, the following will be adjusted pro-rata on a daily basis between Buyer and Seller, reimbursing where applicable current taxes (see Information regarding Real Estate Taxes), rents, interest on mortgage assumptions, condominium fees, and home owners association fees, water and or sewer fees together with any other lienable municipal services.

4:1 Sample Form – Real Estate Purchase Agreement Page 1 Continued

---

1. ***This Agreement***, dated _____ is between SELLER(S):
   _____, called Seller, and
   BUYER(S): _____ , called Buyer.

4:2 Sample Form Extraction – Real Estate Purchase Agreement Page 1

The full names of the buyers and the sellers of the transaction should be included on these lines of the sales agreement.

> If the form of the names varies from the names incorporated into the mortgage application, you must discuss this matter with the borrower. The underwriter will wish to have every individual named on the sales agreement placed on the application and loan.

If any individual is named on the sales agreement but is not included within the application, you must have the name of the extra party removed before the sales agreement is remitted to the underwriting team.

All documents pertinent to the transaction should match in all ways. If there is a discrepancy, you must request correction of the document that contains the error.

---

2. PROPERTY Seller herby agrees to sell and convey to Buyer, who hereby agrees to purchase:
   ALL THAT CERTAIN lot or piece of ground with buildings and improvements thereon erected, if any, known as:
   _____
   _____
   In the _____ of _____ County of _____ in the State of
   _____. Identification (e.g., Tax ID#, Parcel #; Lot, Block; Deed Book, Page,
   Recording Date):

4:3 Sample Form Extraction – Real Estate Purchase Agreement Page 1

The property information should be included on the sales contract.

The description of the property including physical address, city name, county name, and deed information should match all of the other documents in the transaction. If there is a discrepancy, you must request correction of the document that contains the error.

The individual overseeing the file and preparing the documents for closing will use the information entered on these forms to complete the closing package and to generate the signature pages that will close the transaction.

3.   TERMS
     (A) Purchase Price _____
     _____ U.S. Dollars
     which will be paid to the Seller by the Buyer as follows:
        1. Cash or check at the signing of this Agreement_____ $ _____
        2. Cash or check within ____ days of the execution of this agreement_____ $ _____
        3. _____ $ _____
        4. Cash or cashiers check at the time of settlement_____ $ _____
                                                    TOTAL $ _____

4:4 Sample Form Extraction – Real Estate Purchase Agreement Page 1

Purchase Price
The financial details that have been agreed to between the borrower and seller as the basis of the agreement for the sale will be included on the sales agreement.

The purchase entry details the final sales price agreed upon for the transaction.

This figure will act as the basis for all other transaction calculations during the process.

Cash or check at Signing
The area defined as cash or check at the signing of the agreement will be termed the earnest money deposit on your worksheet.

It is important that you review the handling of the earnest money deposit.

The earnest money deposit is a source of borrower funds to close and should be reflected on both the mortgage application and on the good faith estimate.

If these details are not included, you must gain the necessary agreement information in order to have the funds applied correctly as the transaction progresses.

Additional Funds
At times, the buyer and seller may negotiate a transaction in which the buyer pays more than one deposit. If this is the case, the details of these additional payments should be outlined within the contract and the application of the funds should be defined. If these funds are to be allocated to the buyer as part of the process, you will include them in the details of transaction section of your loan package.

Signing Funds   The amount of money that remains due to the seller after the application of all deposit money will be detailed on the sales agreement. You should review these numbers to confirm that all of the funds listed add up to the sales price detailed on the contract. If there is a discrepancy, you should contact the Real Estate Agent if one is being used, or the buyer and seller to have the discrepancy corrected prior to proceeding.

The financial figures entered into the sales agreement will be the ones that you use as the basis for all of the calculations applicable to the transaction. It is essential that the financial basis you use match the sales agreement, as even a slight variation in figures will alter the borrower's debt-to-income ratio, down payment requirements, loan amount, and all other financial estimates.

You should note that these figures only pertain to the actual sales price money for the property. Details pertaining to the closing costs and other financial matters will usually not appear within this section of the sales agreement. The calculation of the remaining costs will be based upon the completion of the good faith estimate and loan structure that your office creates for the borrower.

(B) Deposits paid by Buyer within ____ DAYS of settlement will be by cash or cashiers check. Deposits, regardless of the form of payment and the person designated as payee, will be paid in U.S. Dollars to Broker for Seller (unless otherwise stated here) _____

_____ who will retain deposits in an escrow account until consummation or termination of this Agreement in conformity with all applicable laws and regulations. Any check tendered as deposit monies may be held uncashed pending the acceptance of this agreement.

4:5 Sample Form Extraction – Real Estate Purchase Agreement Page 1

The method of payment, term for payment and handling of the deposit money, both before and after the offer is accepted will be detailed here.

The contingencies pertaining to the application and / or return of the earnest money deposit were explained earlier.

(C) Seller's written approval to be on or before _____
  (D) Settlement to be on _____ or before if Buyer and Seller agree
  (E) Settlement will occur in the county where the Property is located or in an adjacent county, during normal business hours, unless Buyer and Seller agree otherwise.

4:6 Sample Form Extraction – Real Estate Purchase Agreement Page 1

The dates pertinent to the transaction will be included within this section.

The most important date from your prospective will be

"Settlement to be on 'preferred closing date' or before if buyer or seller agree."

The date entered on this line is the date that you will use to manage the flow of the transaction. All applicable actions and documentation should be completed on or before this date so that the transaction can close in compliance with the agreement. If all if the required items cannot be completed by this date, an extension agreement will need to be made between the buyer and the seller.

F)   Conveyance from Seller will be by fee simple deed of Special Warranty unless otherwise stated here _____

4:7 Sample Form Extraction – Real Estate Purchase Agreement Page 1

The specific type of deed that the seller agrees to provide and the buyer agrees to accept will be detailed within the sales agreement.

You should confirm that the type of deed and warranties contained within the deed match the requirements set forth by the underwriting guidelines. The decision to lend money for a specific transaction is contingent on the property specifics as well as the borrower specifics. Any deed limitations could affect the value of the property and would affect the approval terms and loan parameters.

(G)   Payment of transfer taxes will be divided equally between Buyer and Seller unless otherwise stated here _____
_____

(H)   At the time of settlement, the following will be adjusted pro-rata on a daily basis between Buyer and Seller, reimbursing where applicable current taxes (see Information regarding Real Estate Taxes), rents, interest on mortgage assumptions, condominium fees, and home owners association fees, water and or sewer fees together with any other lienable municipal services.

4:8 Sample Form Extraction – Real Estate Purchase Agreement Page 1

The payment of transfer taxes and pro ration calculations pertaining to other costs of the transaction will be detailed within the sales agreement.

You should note

- The division of transaction expenses outlined within the sales contract.

- The date set for the division of fixed expense.

The individual responsible for the preparation of the HUD 1 will calculate and verify the payments incorporated into this clause before finalizing the closing package. A rough estimate of the calculations should be incorporated into the financial details of the 1003 and disclosed on the good faith estimate.

KENNEY

4. **FIXTURES & PERSONAL PROPERTY**
   (A)   INCLUDED in this sale are all existing items, permanently installed in the Property, free of liens, including plumbing, heating, lighting fixtures (including chandeliers and ceiling fans); water treatment systems; pool and spa equipment; garage door openers and transmitters; television antennas; unspotted shrubbery, plantings and trees; any remaining heating and cooking fuels stored on the Property at the time of settlement; sump pumps; storage sheds; mailboxes; wall to wall carpeting; existing window screens, storm windows and screen storm doors, window covering hardware, shades and blinds; awnings; built-in air conditioners, built in appliances; and the range unless otherwise stated. Also included: _____
   (B)   LEASED items (not owned by Seller): _____
   (C)   EXCLUDED fixtures and items: _____

5. **DATES / TIME IS OF THE ESSENCE**
   (A)   The settlement date and all other dates and times referred to for the performance of the obligations of this Agreement are of the essence and are binding.
   (B)   For purposes of this Agreement, the number of days will be counted from the date of execution, excluding the day this Agreement was executed and including the last day of the time period. The Execution Date of this Agreement is the date when Buyer and Seller have indicated full acceptance of this Agreement by signing and/or initialing it. All changes to this Agreement should be initialed and dated.
   (C)   The settlement date is not extended by any other provision of this Agreement and may only be extended by mutual written Agreement of the parties.
   (D)   Certain time periods are pre-printed in this Agreement as a convenience to the Buyer and Seller. All pre-printed time periods are negotiable and may be changed by striking out the pre-printed text and inserting a different time period acceptable to all parties.

6. **MORTGAGE CONTINGENCY**
   __   WAIVED This sales is NOT contingent on mortgage financing, although Buyer may still obtain mortgage financing.
   __   ELECTED
   (A)   The sale is contingent on Buyer obtaining mortgage financing as follows:

First Mortgage on the Property	Second Mortgage on the Property
Loan Amount $_____	Loan Amount $_____
Minimum Term _____ years	Minimum Term _____ years
Type of Mortgage _____	Type of Mortgage _____
Mortgage Lender _____	Mortgage Lender _____
Interest Rate _____% however, Buyer agrees to accept the interest rate as may be committed by the mortgage lender, not to exceed a maximum interest rate of _____%. Discount points, loan origination, loan placement, and other fees charged by the lender as a percentage of the mortgage loan (excluding any mortgage insurance premiums or VA funding fee) not to exceed _____% (1% if not specified)	Interest Rate _____% however, Buyer agrees to accept the interest rate as may be committed by the mortgage lender, not to exceed a maximum interest rate of _____%. Discount points, loan origination, loan placement, and other fees charged by the lender as a percentage of the mortgage loan (excluding any mortgage insurance premiums or VA funding fee) not to exceed _____% (1% if not specified)

The interest rate(s) and fee(s) provisions in paragraph 6(A) are satisfied if the mortgage lender(s) gives Buyer the right to guarantee the interest rate(s) and fee(s) at or before the maximum levels stated. Buyer gives Seller the right at Seller's sole option and as permitted by law and the mortgage lender(s) to contribute financially, without promise of reimbursement to the buyer and or the mortgage lender(s) to make the above mortgage terms available to the Buyer.
   (B)   Within _____ days (10 if not specified) from the Execution Date of this Agreement, Buyer will make a completed, written mortgage application for the mortgage terms stated above to the mortgage lender(s) defined in paragraph 6(A), if any, otherwise to a responsible mortgage lender(s) of Buyer's choice. Broker for Buyer, if any, otherwise Broker for Seller, is authorized to communicate with the mortgage lender(s) to assist in the mortgage loan process.
   (C)   Should Buyer furnish false or incomplete information to Seller, Broker(s), or the mortgage lender(s) concerning Buyer's legal or financial status, or fail to cooperate in good faith in processing the mortgage loan application, which results in the mortgage lender(s) refusing to approve a mortgage loan commitment, Buyer will be in default of this Agreement.
   (D)   1.   Mortgage commitment date: _____ if Seller does not receive a copy of Buyer's mortgage commitment by this date, Buyer and Seller agree to extend the mortgage commitment date until the Seller terminated this Agreement buy written notice to the Buyer
         2.   Upon receiving a mortgage commitment, Buyer will promptly deliver a copy of the commitment to the Seller.
         3.   Seller may terminate this Agreement, in writing, after the mortgage commitment date, if the mortgage commitment
            a.   is not valid until the date of settlement , OR
            b.   is conditional upon the sale and settlement of any other property, OR
            c.   does not satisfy all the mortgage terms as stated in paragraph 6(A), OR
            d.   Contains any other conditions not specified in this Agreement that is not satisfied and or removed in writing by the mortgage lender(s)
         4.   If this Agreement is terminated pursuant to paragraph 6(D)(1) or (3), or the mortgage loan(s) is not obtained for settlement, all deposit monies will be returned to Buyer according to the terms of paragraph 30 and this Agreement will be VOID. Buyer will be responsible for any costs incurred by Buyer for any inspections or certifications obtained according to the terms of this Agreement and any costs incurred by Buyer for (1) Title search, title insurance and or mechanics' lien insurance, or any fee for cancellation. (2) Flood insurance and or fire insurance with extended coverage, mine subsidence insurance or any fee for cancellation (3) Appraisal fee and charges paid in advance to mortgage lender(s)

4:9 Sample Form – Real Estate Purchase Agreement Page 2

---

4.   **FIXTURES & PERSONAL PROPERTY**

 (A)   INCLUDED in this sale are all existing items, permanently installed in the Property, free of liens, including plumbing, heating, lighting fixtures (including chandeliers and ceiling fans); water treatment systems; pool and spa equipment; garage door openers and transmitters; television antennas; unspotted shrubbery, plantings and trees; any remaining heating and cooking fuels stored on the Property at the time of settlement; sump pumps; storage sheds; mailboxes; wall to wall carpeting; existing window screens, storm windows and screen storm doors, window covering hardware, shades and blinds; awnings; built-in air conditioners, built in appliances; and the range unless otherwise stated. Also included: _____

 (B)   LEASED items (not owned by Seller): _____

 (C)   EXCLUDED fixtures and items: _____
 _____

4:10 Sample Form Extraction – Real Estate Purchase Agreement Page 2

Specific details pertaining to the fixtures and personal property that will be included in the sale of the real estate will be shown on the sales agreement. The removal or addition of fixtures and personal property will affect the value of the property and may alter the approval terms of the loan. Many loan guidelines will require the removal of any value assessed to personal property transferring as part of the transaction. This value removal will lower the basis for the loan amount provided to the borrower.

Example: If the sales agreement sets the sales price of a property at $150,000 and the loan approval dictates an eight percent loan to value, the loan amount for the transaction would be $120,000.

The borrower would need to provide the $30,000 shortfall between the sales price and the loan amount as part down payment funds.

If the same sales agreement dictates that the buyer keeps $10,000 worth of furnishings, decorations, and other personal property as part of the negotiations, the value of these items is not a part of the value of the property and underwriting will deduct this value from the overall sales price.

That would mean that the loan amount would now be based on $140,000 ($150,000 sales price - $10,000 furniture and goods = $140,000 property purchase price).

Using the same 80% loan to value, the new loan amount would be $112,000.

The borrower would now need to prove that they have $38,000 to use as down payment funds.

---

5. **DATES / TIME IS OF THE ESSENCE**

   (A)   The settlement date and all other dates and times referred to for the performance of the obligations of this Agreement are of the essence and are binding.
   (B)   For purposes of this Agreement, the number of days will be counted from the date of execution, excluding the day this Agreement was executed and including the last day of the time period. The Execution Date of this Agreement is the date when Buyer and Seller have indicated full acceptance of this Agreement by signing and/or initialing it. All changes to this Agreement should be initialed and dated.
   (C)   The settlement date is not extended by any other provision of this Agreement and may only be extended by mutual written Agreement of the parties.
   (D)   Certain time periods are pre-printed in this Agreement as a convenience to the Buyer and Seller. All pre-printed time periods are negotiable and may be changed by striking out the pre-printed text and inserting a different time period acceptable to all parties.

4:11 Sample Form Extraction – Real Estate Purchase Agreement Page 2

When the sales agreement negotiations are finalized, specific dates for action will be incorporated into the contract.

These dates set the timeline expectations for the transaction.

Some dates are listed based upon industry standard expectations and may be open to negotiation such as the term for a pest inspection.

Other dates are negotiated dates between the buyer and the seller and as such are considered fixed dates that must be met.

If a specifically negotiated date cannot be met for any reason, an alteration to the contract, signed by all parties, must be created. This type of date includes items such as the mortgage application and approval dates and the expected close date.

It is very important that you use these dates to set the timeline for the transaction and ensure that all required activity is finalized by the expected close date. Additional details pertaining to the expected time flow of a transaction and potential delays to the closing date and methods that you may use to overcome these potential delays are included later in the course.

---

6. **MORTGAGE CONTINGENCY**

   ___   WAIVED This sales is NOT contingent on mortgage financing, although Buyer may still obtain mortgage financing.
   ___   ELECTED

4:12 Sample Form Extraction – Real Estate Purchase Agreement Page 2

The borrower may elect to incorporate a mortgage contingency clause into the sales agreement. This clauses states that the offer to purchase is contingent on your offices ability to structure a loan that enables the borrower to purchase the property. The mortgage contingency clause is one of the most common reasons that an offer to purchase will be cancelled. It is critical that you ensure that you complete all of the functions related to the obtainment of the mortgage in a timely manner and in compliance with the terms set forth in the sales agreement.

First Mortgage on the Property	Second Mortgage on the Property
Loan Amount $_____	Loan Amount $_____
Minimum Term _____ years	Minimum Term _____ years
Type of Mortgage _____ _____	Type of Mortgage _____ _____
Mortgage Lender _____	Mortgage Lender _____
Interest Rate _____% however, Buyer agrees to accept the interest rate as may be committed by the mortgage lender, not to exceed a maximum interest rate of _____%. Discount points, loan origination, loan placement, and other fees charged by the lender as a percentage of the mortgage loan (excluding any mortgage insurance premiums or VA funding fee) not to exceed _____% (1% if not specified)	Interest Rate _____% however, Buyer agrees to accept the interest rate as may be committed by the mortgage lender, not to exceed a maximum interest rate of _____%. Discount points, loan origination, loan placement, and other fees charged by the lender as a percentage of the mortgage loan (excluding any mortgage insurance premiums or VA funding fee) not to exceed _____% (1% if not specified)

4:13 Sample Form Extraction – Real Estate Purchase Agreement Page 2

Specific parameters under which the buyer may decline mortgage funding or must accept mortgage funding will often be included in the sales agreement. The minimum and maximum terms of the mortgage that the borrower believes will be acceptable will be outlined. You should review this clause and compare it to the financing that the borrower may actually obtain. If there is a discrepancy between the approval that the borrower receives and the terms outlined in the sales agreement, the sales contract may need to be modified. This modification of the borrower's expectations ensures that the mortgage clause matches the true loan terms and limits the probability that the transaction will be cancelled later in the process. A late cancellation can be expensive to all of the parties involved and will be frustrating to you because you will have invested a great deal of time and effort into the completion of the loan package.

Timelines for application and approval of mortgage funding will be included in the contract. These dates will assist you in setting the time flow and activity sheets for the application remittal, documentation needs, and other preparations you must undertake to meet the expected close date.

Additional details that may be applicable to your transaction such as costs, fees, and other matters may be incorporated. Any detail included within the sales agreement under the mortgage contingency clause should be transferred to your loan package.

KENNEY

(E) If the mortgage lender(s), or an insurer providing property and casualty insurance s required by the mortgage lender(s), requires repairs to the Property, Buyer will, upon receiving the requirements, deliver a copy of the requirements to the Seller. Within ___ DAYS of receiving the copy of the requirements, Seller will notify Buyer whether Seller will make the required repairs at Seller's expense.

  1. If Seller makes the required repairs to the satisfaction of the mortgage lender(s) or insurer, Buyer accepts the Property and agrees to the RELEASE in paragraph 27 of this Agreement.
  2. If Seller will not make the required repairs, or if Seller fails to respond within the time given, Buyer will, within ___ days, notify Seller of Buyer's choice to:
    a. Make the required repairs, at Buyer's expense, with permission and access to the Property given by Seller; permission and access may not be unreasonably withheld by Seller, OR
    b. Terminate this Agreement by written notice to Seller, with all deposit monies returned to Buyer according ot the terms of paragraph 30 of this Agreement.

(F) **Seller Assist**
  __ NOT APPLICABLE
  __ APPLICABLE, Seller will pay:
    $_____, or _____% of Purchase Price, maximum, toward Buyer's costs as acceptable to the mortgage lender(s)

FHA/VA, IF APPLIABLE

(G) It is expressly agreed that notwithstanding any other provisions of this contract, Buyer will not be obligated to complete the purchase of the Property described herein or to incur any penalty by forfeiture of earnest money deposits or otherwise unless Buyer has been given, in accordance with HUD/FHA or VA requirements, a written statement by the Federal Housing Commissioner, Veterans Administration, or a Direct Endorsement Lender setting forth the appraised value of the Property of not less than $_____ (the dollar amount to be inserted is the sales price as stated in this Agreement). Buyer will have the privilege and option of proceeding with consummation of the contract without regard to the amount of the appraised valuation. The appraised valuation is arrived at to determine the maximum mortgage the Department of Housing and Urban Development will insure. HUD does not warrant the value nor the condition of the Property as acceptable.
Warning: Section 1010 of Title 18, U.S.C., Department of Housing and Urban Development and Federal Housing Administration Transactions, provides, "Whoever for the purpose of... influencing in any way the action of such Department, makes, passes, utters or publishes any statement, knowing the same to be false... shall be fined under this title or imprisoned not more than two years or both."

(H) **U.S. Department of Housing and Urban Development (HUD) NOTICE TO PURCHASERS: Buyer's Acknowledgement**
  __ Buyer has received the HUD Notice "For Your Protection: Get a Home Inspection." Buyer understands the importance of getting an independent home inspection and has thought about this before signing this Agreement. Buyer understands that FHA will not perform a home inspection nor guarantee the price or condition of the Property.

(I) **Certification** We the undersigned, Seller(s) and Buyer(s) party to this transaction each certify that the terms of this contract for purchase are true to the best of our knowledge and believe, and that any other agreement entered into by any of these parties in connection with this transaction is attached to this Agreement.

7. **WAIVER OF CONTINGENCIES**
If this Agreement is contingent on Buyer's right to inspect and/or repair the Property, or to verify insurability, environmental conditions, boundaries, certifications, zoning classification or use, or any other information regarding the Property, Buyer's failure to exercise any of Buyer's options within the times set forth in this Agreement is a WAIVER of that contingency and Buyer accepts the Property and agrees to the RELEASE in paragraph 27 of this Agreement.

8. **PROPERTY INSURANCE AVAILABILITY**
  __ WAIVED. This Agreement is NOT contingent upon Buyer obtaining property and casualty insurance for the Property, although Buyer may still obtain property and casualty insurance.
  __ ELECTED. Contingency Period: ___ DAYS (15 if not specified) from the Execution Date of this Agreement.
  Within the Contingency Period, Buyer will make application for property and casualty insurance for the Property to a responsible insurer. **Broker for Buyer, if any, otherwise Broker for Seller, may communicate with the insurer to assist in the insurance process**. If Buyer cannot obtain property and casualty insurance for the Property on terms and conditions reasonably acceptable to Buyer, Buyer will, within the Contingency Period:
  (A) Accept the Property and agree to the RELEASE in paragraph 27 of this Agreement, OR
  (B) Terminate this Agreement by written notice to Seller, with all deposit monies returned to Buyer according to the terms of paragraph 30 of this Agreement, OR
  (C) Enter into a mutually acceptable written agreement with Seller.
  If Buyer and Seller do not reach a written agreement during the Contingency Period, and Buyer does not terminate this Agreement by written notice to Seller within that time, Buyer will accept the Property and agree to the RELEASE in paragraph 27 of this Agreement.

9. **INSPECTIONS**
  (A) Seller will provide access to insurers' representatives and, as may be required by this Agreement, to surveyors, municipal officials, and inspectors. If Buyer is obtaining mortgage financing, Seller will provide access to the Property to appraisers and others reasonably required by the mortgage lender(s). Buyer may attend any inspections.

4:14 Sample Form– Real Estate Purchase Agreement Page 3

(E) If the mortgage lender(s), or an insurer providing property and casualty insurance s required by the mortgage lender(s), requires repairs to the Property, Buyer will, upon receiving the requirements, deliver a copy of the requirements to the Seller. Within ___ DAYS of receiving the copy of the requirements, Seller will notify Buyer whether Seller will make the required repairs at Seller's expense.
  1. If Seller makes the required repairs to the satisfaction of the mortgage lender(s) or insurer, Buyer accepts the Property and agrees to the RELEASE in paragraph 27 of this Agreement.
  2. If Seller will not make the required repairs, or if Seller fails to respond within the time given, Buyer will, within ___ days, notify Seller of Buyer's choice to:
  a. Make the required repairs, at Buyer's expense, with permission and access to the Property given by Seller; permission and access may not be unreasonably withheld by Seller, OR
  b. Terminate this Agreement by written notice to Seller, with all deposit monies returned to Buyer according ot the terms of paragraph 30 of this Agreement.

4:13 Sample Form Extraction – Real Estate Purchase Agreement Page 3

The loan commitment provided by underwriting will detail any repairs that must be made to the property in order for the loan to be completed. These repairs are typically based on the inclusions and descriptions contained within the appraisal report and will include any matter that must be remedied in order to stabilize the value and condition of the property.

If such stipulations exist, you must ensure that the borrower negotiates an addendum to the sales contract that dictates who will make said repairs and bear the cost of the repairs.

(F) **Seller Assist**
  __ NOT APPLICABLE
  __ APPLICABLE, Seller will pay:
       $_____, or _____% of Purchase Price, maximum, toward Buyer's costs as acceptable to the mortgage lender(s)
       _____

4:14 Sample Form Extraction – Real Estate Purchase Agreement Page 3

The practice of requesting assistance toward the payment of closing costs from the seller in a transaction is becoming more common.

> Many standard real estate sales agreements have incorporated a specific clause pertaining to this negotiation.

> Seller concessions are the specific amount of funds a seller will allocate toward paying buyers closing costs out of the sellers closing proceeds.

The amount of seller assistance must comply with the maximum amount set forth in the underwriting guidelines for the loan program. Many programs have maximum amounts of seller assistance that they will allow.

If seller assistance is incorporated into the sales agreement, these figures should be included within the financial details section of the ten o three. Any financial modification that you make to the ten o three will carry with it a requirement that you remit the application package to the underwriter so that they may review and approve the changes.

Many borrowers require assistance in obtaining all of the required funds for closing and seller assistance is one tool that will enable the borrower to secure adequate funds. It is important that you understand that seller assistance funds come from the transaction. What this means is that the funds appear as a credit from the seller, but the money used will actually come from the loan funds and down payment money that the borrower brings to the table.

You should verify all of the seller assistance details, allowed costs offsets, and the inclusion of such assistance on the HUD 1 prior to beginning the settlement meeting. All of the entries relating to closing cost assistance must comply with the requirements of the loan guidelines. If any wording or allocation agreement relating to the closing cost assistance does not meet the requirements of the loan guidelines, the sales agreement will need to be modified to bring the negotiations into line with the mortgage approval terms.

At times, errors in the calculations or application of the seller assistance funds can occur during the preparation of the closing documents. It is important that all allowable seller assistance be credited to the borrower at the closing and that the assistance is credited in the correct location on the HUD 1.

Example: The loan guidelines dictate that the seller assistance may be applied to non-recurring closing costs, the allocation of seller assistance on the HUD 1 must be in entries related to non-recurring closing costs.

If the closing agent preparing the settlement statement was to enter some of the seller assistance money in the area detailing payment for homeowners insurance a problem may arise that delays the closing.

Homeowner's insurance premiums are recurring closing costs.

The entry of the seller assistance funds in this area may cause underwriting to invalidate the transaction until the funds are applied according to the guidelines.

The ability to review all documentation before the commencement of closing will enable you to isolate and correct issues before the parties arrive to close the transaction. Gaining a reputation for processing loan packages that lead to a smooth closing is one element that will assist you in growing your business and ensuring referral business from each loan that you close.

Certain specific inspections of the property may be written into the agreement. It is important for you to know some basic facts pertaining to these inspections. You will need to locate the

- Information detailing who will pay for the inspection

- And the specific agreement regarding when the payment for the inspections will be made

The payment for any required inspections may be made outside of closing or these payments may become part of the closing costs paid at the settlement meeting.

All billings pertaining to the transaction that are not paid prior to close must be addressed at the closing table so that the transaction may close without additional obligations coming to the surface for either the buyer or the seller at some point in the future.

When inspections are completed, specific items may become known that must be addressed or corrected prior to the closing of the loan.

Example: If a termite inspection is completed and termites are found on the subject property, one party will likely be responsible for having the problems relating to the termites corrected.

This could cause closing delays while the problem is corrected.

Any matter that must be corrected may also result in additional costs.

The handling of deficiencies should be written into the contracts and all inspections should be ordered early in the loan process. Addressing these items early helps to ensure that there is adequate time to remedy any issues that are discovered.

10. INSPECTION CONTINGENCY OPTIONS

The inspection contingencies elected by Buyer in paragraphs 11-15 are controlled by the Options set forth below. The time periods in these Options will apply to all inspection contingencies in paragraphs 11-15 unless otherwise stated in this Agreement.

Option 1. Within the Contingency Period, as stated in paragraphs 11-15, Buyer will:
1. Accept the Property with the information stated in the report(s) and agree to the RELEASE in paragraph 27 of this Agreement, OR
2. If Buyer is not satisfied with the information stated in the report(s), terminate this Agreement by written notice to the Seller, with all deposit monies returned to the Buyer according to the terms of paragraph 30 of this Agreement, OR
3. Enter into a mutually acceptable written agreement with the Seller providing for any repairs or improvements to the Property and or any credit to Buyer at settlement, as acceptable to the mortgage lender(s), if any.

If Buyer and Seller do not reach a written agreement during the specified Contingency Period, an Buyer does not terminate this Agreement by written notice to Seller within that time, Buyer will accept the Property and agree to the RELEASE in paragraph 27 of this Agreement.

Option 2. Within the Contingency Period, as stated in paragraphs 11-15, Buyer will:
1. Accept the Property with the information stated in the report(s) and agree to the RELEASE in paragraph 27 of this Agreement, OR
2. If Buyer is not satisfied with the information stated in the report(s), present the report(s) to Seller with a Written Corrective Proposal ("Proposal") listing corrections and/or credits desired by Buyer. The Proposal may, but is not required to, include the name of a properly licensed or qualified professional to perform the corrections requested in the Proposal, provisions for payment, including retests, and a projected date for completion of the corrections. Buyer agrees that Seller will not be held liable for corrections that do not comply with mortgage lender or governmental requirements if performed in a workmanlike manner according to the terms of Buyer's Proposal, or by a contractor selected by Buyer.
   a. Within ___ days (7 if not specified) of receiving Buyer's Proposal, Seller will inform Buyer in writing of Seller's choice to:
      1. Satisfy the terms of Buyer's Proposal, OR
      2. Credit Buyer at settlement for the cost to satisfy the terms of Buyer's Proposal, as acceptable to mortgage lender(s), if any, OR
      3. Not satisfy the terms of Buyer's Proposal or to credit Buyer at settlement for the costs to satisfy the terms of Buyer's Proposal.
   b. If Seller agrees to satisfy the terms of Buyer's Proposal or to credit Buyer at settlement as specified above, Buyer accepts Property and agrees to the RELEASE in paragraph 27 of this Agreement.
   c. If seller chooses not to satisfy the terms of Buyer's Proposal and not to credit Buyer at settlement as specified above, of if Seller fails to choose any option within the time give, Buyer will within ___ days (5 if not specified);
      1. Accept the Property with the information stated in the report(s) and agree to the RELEASE in paragraph 27 of this Agreement, OR
      2. Terminate this Agreement by written notice to Seller, with all deposit monies returned to Buyer according to the terms of paragraph 30 of this Agreement, OR
      3. Enter into a mutually acceptable written agreement with Seller providing for any repairs or improvements to the Property and/or any credit to Buyer at settlement, as acceptable to the mortgage lender(s) if any.

11. **PROPERTY INSPECTION CONTINGENCY** (See Property and Environmental Inspection Notices)

Buyer understands that property inspections, certifications and/or investigations can be performed by professional contractors, home inspectors, engineers, architects and other properly licensed or otherwise qualified professionals, and may include, but are not limited to: structural components; roof; exterior windows and exterior doors; exterior siding, fascia, gutters and downspouts; swimming pools, hot tubs and spas; appliances; electrical, plumbing, heating and cooling systems; water penetration; environmental hazards (e.g., mold, fungi, indoor air quality, asbestos, underground storage tanks, etc.); electromagnetic fields; wetlands inspection; flood plain verification; property boundary/square footage verification; and any other items Buyer may select. Buyer is advised to investigate easements, deed and use restrictions (including any historic preservation restrictions or ordinances) that apply to the Property and to review local zoning ordinances. Other provisions of this Agreement may provide for inspections, certifications and/or investigations that are not waived or altered by Buyer's election here.

___ WAIVED Buyer has the option to conduct property inspections, certifications, and/or investigations. Buyer WAIVES THIS OPTION and agrees to the RELEASE in paragraph 27 of this agreement.

___ ELECTED Contingency Period: ___ days (15 if not specified) from the Execution Date of this Agreement.

(A) Within the Contingency Period, Buyer, at Buyer's expense, may have inspections, certifications and/or investigations completed by properly licensed or otherwise qualified professionals. If Buyer elects to have a home inspection of the Property, as defined in the Pennsylvania Home Inspection Law (see Information Regarding the Home Inspection Law), the home inspection must be performed by a full member of a national home inspection association, in accordance with the ethical standards and code of conduct or practice of that association, or by a properly licensed or registered professional engineer, or a properly licensed or registered architect. This contingency does not apply to the following conditions or items: _____

(B) If Buyer is not satisfied with the condition of the Property as stated in the written inspection report(s), Buyer will proceed under one of the following Options as listed in paragraph 10 within the Contingency Period:

___ Option 1

___ Option 2 For the purposes of Paragraph 11 only, Buyer agrees to accept the Property with the results of any report(s) and agrees to the RELEASE in paragraph 27 of this Agreement if the total cost to correct the conditions stated in the report(s) is less than $_____ ($0 if not specified) (the "Deductible Amount"). Otherwise, all provisions of paragraph 10, Option 2, shall apply, except that Seller will be deemed to have satisfied the terms of Buyer's Proposal if Seller agrees to perform corrections or offer credits such that the cumulative cost of any uncorrected or uncredited condition(s) is equal to the Deductible Amount.

2. WOOD INFESTATION INSPECTION CONTINGENCY

___ WAIVED. Buyer has the option to have the Property inspected for wood infestation by an inspector certified as a wood-destroying pests pesticide applicator. BUYER WAIVES THIS OPTOIN and agrees to the RELEASE in paragraph 27 of this Agreement.

___ ELECTED. Contingency Period ___ days (15 if not specified) from the Execution Date of this Agreement.

(A) Within the Contingency Period, Buyer, at Buyer's expense, may obtain a written "Wood Destroying Insect Infestation Inspection Report" from an inspector certified as a wood-destroying pests pesticide applicator and will deliver it an all supporting documents and drawings provided by the inspector to Seller. The report is to be made satisfactory to and in compliance with applicable laws, mortgage lender requirements, and/or Federal Insuring and Guaranteeing Agency requirements, if any. The inspection is to be limited to all readily visible and accessible areas of all structures on the Property except fences and the following structures, which will not be inspected:

_____

(B) If the inspection reveals active infestation(s), Buyer, at Buyer's expense, may within the Contingency Period, obtain a proposal from a wood-destroying pests pesticide applicator to treat the Property.

(C) If the inspection reveals damage from active or previous infestation(s), Buyer, at Buyer's expense, may within the Contingency Period, obtain a written report from a professional contractor, home inspector, or structural engineer that is limited to structural damage to the Property caused by wood-destroying organisms and a Proposal to repair and/or treat the Property.

(D) If Buyer is not satisfied with the condition of the Property as stated in the written inspection report(s), Buyer will proceed under one of the following Options as listed in paragraph 10 within the Contingency Period:
  ___ Option 1
  ___ Option 2

3. STATUS OF RADON

(A) Seller has no knowledge concerning the presence or absence of radon unless checked below:

  ___ 1. Seller has knowledge that the Property was tested on the dates, by the methods (e.g., charcoal canister, alpha track, etc.), and with the results of the test indicated below:
  DATE   TYPE OF TEST   RESULTS (picocuries/liter or working levels)

  _____
  ___ 2. Seller has knowledge that the Property underwent radon reduction measures on the date(s) and by the method(s) indicated below:
  DATE   RADON REDUCTION METHOD

  _____
  COPIES OF ALL AVAILABLE TEST REPORTS will be delivered to Buyer with this Agreement. SELLER DOES NOT WARRANT EITHER THE METHODS OR RESULTS OF THE TESTS.

(B) RADON INSPECTION CONTINGENCY

  ___ WAIVED. Buyer has the option to have the Property inspected for radon by a certified inspector. BUYER WAIVES THIS OPTION and agrees to the RELEASE in paragraph 27 of this Agreement.

  ___ ELECTED. Contingency Period: ____ Days (15 if not specified) from the Execution Date of this Agreement.
  Within the Contingency Period, Buyer, at Buyer's expense, may obtain a radon test a radon test of the Property from a certified inspector. If Seller performs any radon remediation, Seller will provide Buyer a certification that the remediation was performed by a properly licensed and certified radon mitigation company.
  1. If the written test report reveals the presence of radon below 0.02 working levels or 4 picoCuries/liter(4 pCi/L), Buyer accepts the Property and agrees to the RELEASE in paragraph 27 of this Agreement.
  2. If the written test report reveals the presence of radon at or exceeding 0.02 working levels or 4 picoCuries/liter (4 pCi/L), Buyer will proceed under one of the following options as listed in paragraph 10 within the Contingency Period.
    ___ Option 1
    ___ Option 2

4. STAUTS OF WATER

(A) Seller represents that the Property is served by:
  ___   Public Water
  ___   On-site Water
  ___   Community Water
  ___   None

  _____

(B) WATER SERVICE INSPECTION CONTINGENCY

  ___ WAIVED. Buyer has the option to have an inspection of the quality and or quantity of the water system for the Property. BUYER WAIVES THIS OPTION and agrees to the RELEASE in paragraph 27 of this Agreement.

  ___ ELECTED. Contingency Period ___ days (15 if not specified) from the Execution Date of this Agreement.
  1. Within the Contingency Period, Buyer, at Buyer's expense, may obtain an inspection of the quality and/or quantity of the water system from a properly licensed or otherwise qualified water/well testing company.
  2. If required by the inspection company, Seller, at Seller's expense, will locate and provide access to the on-site (or individual) water system. Seller also agrees to restore the Property, at Seller's expense, prior to settlement.
  3. If Buyer is not satisfied with the condition of the water system as stated in the written inspection report(s), Buyer will proceed under one of the following options as listed in paragraph 10 within the Contingency Period:
    ___Option 1
    ___Option 2

4:16 Sample Form– Real Estate Purchase Agreement Page 6

KENNEY

(C) In the event any notices (including violations) and/or assessments are received after Seller has signed this Agreement and before settlement, Seller will provide a copy of the notices and/or assessments to Buyer and will notify Buyer in writing within ___ days after receiving the notices and/or assessments that seller will:
  1. Fully comply with the notices and/or assessments at Seller's expense before settlement. If Seller fully complies with the notices and/or assessments, Buyer accepts the Property and agrees to the RELEASE in paragraph 27 of this Agreement OR
  2. Not comply with the notices and/or assessments. If Seller chooses not to comply with the notices and/or assessments, or fails within the time given to notify Buyer whether Seller will comply, Buyer will notify Seller in writing within ___ days that Buyer will:
     a. Comply with the notices and/or assessments at Buyer's expense, accept the Property, and agree to the RELEASE in paragraph 27 of this Agreement OR
     b. Terminate this Agreement by written notice to Seller, with all deposit monies returned to Buyer according to the terms of paragraph 30 of this Agreement.
     If Buyer fails to respond within the time stated in paragraph 18 (C) (2) or fails to terminate this Agreement by written notice to the Seller within that time, Buyer will accept the Property and agree to the RELEASE in paragraph 27 of this Agreement.
(D) If required by law, within ___ DAYS From the Execution Date of this Agreement, but in no case later than 15 days prior to settlement, Seller will order at Seller's expense a certification from the appropriate municipal department(s) disclosing notice of any uncorrected violations of zoning, housing, building, safety, or fire ordinances and/or a certificate permitting occupancy of the Property. If Buyer receives notice of any required repairs/improvements, Buyer will promptly deliver a copy of the notice to the Seller.
  1. Within ___ DAYS of receiving notice form the municipality that repairs/improvements are required, Seller will notify Buyer in writing that the Seller will:
     a. Make the required repairs/improvements to the satisfaction of the municipality. If Seller makes the require repairs/improvements, Buyer accepts the Property and agrees to the RELEASE in paragraph 27 of this Agreement OR
     b. Not make the required repairs/improvements. If Seller chooses not to make the required repairs/improvements, Buyer will notify Seller in writing within ___ DAYS that Buyer will:
        (1) Make the repairs/improvements at Buyer's expense, with permission and access to the Property given by Seller, which will not be unreasonably withheld, OR
        (2) Terminate this Agreement by written notice to Seller, with all deposit monies returned to Buyer according to the terms of paragraph 30 of this Agreement.
        If Buyer fails to respond within the time stated in paragraph 18 (D) (1) (b) or fails to terminate this Agreement by written notice to Seller within that time, Buyer will accept the Property and agree to the RELEASE in paragraph 27 of this Agreement, and Buyer accepts the responsibility to perform the repairs/improvements according to the terms of the notice provided by the municipality.
  2. If Seller denies Buyer permission to make the required repairs/improvements, or does not provide Buyer access before settlement to make the required repairs/improvements, Buyer may, within ___ DAYS, terminate this Agreement by written notice to Seller, with all deposit monies returned to Buyer according to paragraph 30 of this Agreement
  3. If repairs/improvements are required and Seller fails to provide a copy of the notice to Buyer as required in paragraph 18 (D), Seller will perform all repairs/improvements as required by the notice at Seller's expense. Paragraph 18(D)(3) will survive settlement.
19. TITLE, SURVEYS & COSTS
  (A) The Property will be conveyed with good and marketable title as is insurable by a reputable title company at the regular rates, free and clear of all liens, encumbrances, and easements, EXCEPTING HOWEVER the following: existing deed restrictions; historic preservation restrictions or ordinances; building restrictions; ordinances; easements of roads; easements visible upon the ground; easements of record; and privileges or rights of public service companies, if any.
  (B) Buyer will pay for the following: (1) Title search, title insurance and/or mechanics' lien insurance, or any fee for cancellation; (2) Flood insurance, fire insurance with extended coverage, mine subsidence insurance, or any fee for cancellation; (3) Appraisal fees and charges paid in advance to mortgage lender(s); (4) Buyer's customary settlement costs and accruals.
  (C) Any survey or surveys required by the title insurance company or abstracting attorney for preparing an adequate legal description of the Property (or the correction thereof) will be obtained and paid for by Seller. Any survey or surveys desired by Buyer or required by the mortgage lender will be obtained and paid for by Buyer.
  (D) If Seller is unable to give a good and marketable title and such as is insurable by a reputable title insurance company at the regular rates, as specified in paragraph 19 (A), Buyer will:
    1. Accept the Property with such title as Seller can give, with no change to the purchase price, and agree to the RELEASE in paragraph 27 of this Agreement, OR
    2. Terminate this Agreement by written notice to Seller, with all deposit monies to Buyer according to the terms of paragraph 30 of this Agreement. Upon termination, Seller will reimburse Buyer for any costs incurred by Buyer for any inspections or certifications obtained according to the terms of this Agreement, and for those items specified in paragraph 19 (B) items (1), (2), (3) and in paragraph 19 (C).
  (E) The property is not a "recreational cabin" as defined in the Pennsylvania Construction Code Act unless otherwise stated here (see information regarding Recreational Cabins): _____
20. CONDOMINIUM/PLANNED COMMUNITY (HOMEOWNER ASSOCIATION) RESALE NOTICE
  __ NOT APPLICABLE
  __ APPLICABLE

4:16 Sample Form– Real Estate Purchase Agreement Page 7

---

19. **TITLE, SURVEYS & COSTS**

(A) The Property will be conveyed with good and marketable title as is insurable by a reputable title company at the regular rates, free and clear of all liens, encumbrances, and easements, EXCEPTING HOWEVER the following: existing deed restrictions; historic preservation restrictions or ordinances; building restrictions; ordinances; easements of roads; easements visible upon the ground; easements of record; and privileges or rights of public service companies, if any.

(B) Buyer will pay for the following: (1) Title search, title insurance and/or mechanics' lien insurance, or any fee for cancellation; (2) Flood insurance, fire insurance with extended coverage, mine subsidence insurance, or any fee for cancellation; (3) Appraisal fees and charges paid in advance to mortgage lender(s); (4) Buyer's customary settlement costs and accruals.

(C) Any survey or surveys required by the title insurance company or abstracting attorney for preparing an adequate legal description of the Property (or the correction thereof) will be obtained and paid for by Seller. Any survey or surveys desired by Buyer or required by the mortgage lender will be obtained and paid for by Buyer.

(D) If Seller is unable to give a good and marketable title and such as is insurable by a reputable title insurance company at the regular rates, as specified in paragraph 19 (A), Buyer will:

1. Accept the Property with such title as Seller can give, with no change to the purchase price, and agree to the RELEASE in paragraph 27 of this Agreement, OR
2. Terminate this Agreement by written notice to Seller, with all deposit monies to Buyer according to the terms of paragraph 30 of this Agreement. Upon termination, Seller will reimburse Buyer for any costs incurred by Buyer for any inspections or certifications obtained according to the terms of this Agreement, and for those items specified in paragraph 19 (B) items (1), (2), (3) and in paragraph 19 (C).

(E) The property is not a "recreational cabin" as defined in the Pennsylvania Construction Code Act unless otherwise stated here (see information regarding Recreational Cabins): _____

4:17 Sample Form Extraction – Real Estate Purchase Agreement Page 7

Specific terms relating to

- The marketability of the title

- The ability to insure the title

- Restrictions specific to the property

- Easements, rights and privileges pertaining to the property

- The costs pertaining to the searching and insuring the title

- Survey completion and costs

may be incorporated into the sales agreement. If any item cannot be met according to the contract, the options available to the parties should be outlined.

These terms should be verified, specifically those relating to the party who will bear the costs associated with each of these contingency clauses. If any question exists pertaining to which party will pay for the costs associated with any clause, you should contact the buyer, seller or real estate agent to obtain a formalized agreement between the parties prior to completing the financial calculations of the transaction. The payment of these items could affect the loan terms, approval, and cash required from the borrower to complete the process.

Details regarding possession of the property as well as any lease assignments relating to the property should be incorporated into the sales agreement. Many standard agreements contain a clause that provides default instructions for a transaction. Any alteration to this clause would appear in an addendum to the contract. You should confirm the specific negotiations pertaining to possession. If possession is to occur at some point in the future or is based upon an unusual negotiation, you should confirm that these occupancy options meet with the approval guidelines of the loan. Approval is often based on the occupancy plans that the borrower has for the property with owner-occupied property being approved for a higher loan to value than non-owner occupied property. Any change to the planned or agreed upon occupancy of the property could create a delay during the underwriting processes or even result in a change to the loan to value approval status of the borrower.

Details regarding the earnest money deposit, the application of the deposit toward costs, and the specifics of how or when the buyer may regain or loose rights to the earnest money deposit should be outlined within the contract.

Standard contracts typically contain a specific clause dealing with the earnest money deposit, but these standard clauses can be altered through additions to the contract or by addendums to the sales agreement. Non-standard contracts should specify the pertinent handling of earnest money funds.

The handling of the earnest money deposit and method of applying this deposit will be important to the loan structure process, the sourcing of down payment money, and the calculation of the cash the borrower will need to bring to the closing table.

Other conditions or contingencies may be written into the sales agreement. Any item that is of concern or interest to either party may become part of the agreement for transfer. You should review the entire contract, addendums and other paperwork remitted to your office to gain a better understanding of the unique details in each transaction. As you can see, the specifics of the transaction will alter the methodology, details, and handling of the loan package and gaining a complete understanding of each potential alteration will benefit you by making closings a smoother process for all parties.

Chapter

5

BASIC LOAN PROCESS

You will establish your own personal system for fulfilling all the myriad of tasks involved with a loan process from initial contact to closing the loan. The loan officer with whom you work will have other specific methods they choose to use in the loan process. A large portion of the loan processor day will be spent moving the loan process toward a speedy closing. The more organized you become at incorporating all of the necessary tasks into your workflow the more vital to the office you will become.

To aid you in creating your own loan system, we have created a process overview that encompasses the required tasks in a timely manner.

Complete the Pre-Qualification
Questionnaire

You will need to have the Pre-Qualification forms available at all times, preferably bound in a reference Binder.

Pull Credit

Pull the Credit report for both the borrower and the co borrower.

Review Credit Report

The review of the credit report is typically completed by the Loan Officer. As you gain in knowledge and skills, the task of reviewing the credit report may become one of your duties. Reviewing the credit report is typically an advanced processing task. If you feel comfortable with the basics of loan processing, you may wish to consider obtaining training in processor advancement skills so that you can become even more proficient at your chosen profession and more valuable to the loan office.

For now, the loan officer will provide you with a copy of the completed credit review form. This form will enable you to note additional documentation requirements that the borrower may need to provide because of an entry on the credit report.

Qualify loan

This task is typically completed by the loan officer. You should provide all the applicable forms and documents to the loan officer so that they may begin planning the loan strategy. If you feel comfortable with the basics of loan processing, you may wish to consider obtaining training in processor advancement skills so that you can become even more proficient at your chosen profession and more valuable to the loan office.

For now, you will provide the loan officer with all of the applicable forms necessary to begin qualifying the loan package, these include the

> Pre-Qualification Questionnaire
>
> Credit Report
>
> D. T. I. Ratio Form
>
> Credit History Form

Screen for possible programs

The loan officer will compare the borrower profile with the requirements of the different loan programs to choose a loan offering for the borrower. The loan officer will have the applicable lender matrix and guideline manuals available for their use.

If you feel comfortable with the basics of loan processing, you may wish to consider obtaining training in processor advancement skills so that you can become even more proficient at your chosen profession and more valuable to the loan office.

Rate/Price Loan

Once the loan officer has chosen a loan program suitable for the borrower's goals and whose guidelines fit the profile of the borrower, the loan officer will determine a Rate and Price basis for the loan. If you feel comfortable with the basics of loan processing, you may wish to consider obtaining training in processor advancement skills so that you can become even more proficient at your chosen profession and more valuable to the loan office.

For now, you must ensure that the loan officer has all of the necessary documents, manuals, and forms required to complete the pricing tasks. To price the loan, the loan officer will need all of the documents from the loan file and the Product Matrix for the chosen loan product and the most up to date rate sheet for the loan program being considered. You should ensure that these items are available to the loan officer so that the pricing tasks can be accomplished quickly.

This task is typically completed by the loan officer. The loan officer will have the applicable forms and documents available.

> Product Matrix
>
> Rate Sheet
>
> Worksheets

Set Appointment/ Request Documentation

Once the loan officer has completed their tasks on the loan file, they will typically return the package to you so that you can contact the borrower to set an appointment for the completion of the application and obtainment of file documents.

You will request documentation based on the guidelines of the loan program that has been chosen for the borrower and on the borrower's specific situation.

You will nearly always request that the borrower bring

- 2 years W-2s,

- Year To Date pay stubs

  The borrower should bring pay stubs that cover the full 30 day period prior to the meeting.

- If the borrower rents from an individual rather than an entity, you should request 12 months proof of timely rental payments in the form of rent checks.

- Credit Documents

- Contested Items

- Divorce Decree etc

- Any additional items you feel may be requested by underwriting based on information on Pre-qualification Questionnaire and Credit report

Appointment

Once the preliminary file assessment, loan planning, and documentation list is created, you will contact the borrower and set an Appointment for the application meeting.

The loan officer will typically be the one who conducts the application meeting, but it will be a part of your function to ensure that the borrower understands what documentation they must bring to the meeting.

You should ensure that the loan file contains all of the necessary data, disclosure forms, and application materials that the loan officer will need during the meeting.

Once the application meeting is complete, you will receive the file back for review and submittal. You should review all of the documents contained in the loan file before submitting the package to underwriting.

If any discrepancies exist on the file, you will need to bring it to the loan officer's attention so that corrections can be made before the submittal.

Stack Loan Package

You will stack the submittal items according to the preferences of the particular lender to whom the package is being directed. You will use the underwriting checklist or Submittal summary Form to ensure that the documents are stacked correctly and that all of the necessary items are included.

If the borrower is completing the application by mail or telephone, you will mail the required signature documents and disclosures to the borrower.

You may be required to create a loan cover letter for the borrower. You should carefully review the loan file to ensure that you have an understanding of the plans the loan officer has made with and for the borrower. If you have any questions regarding the file, you should confer with the loan officer before completing the loan cover letter. Remember, the initial submittal is the time to set the stage with underwriting. The cover letter should contain a brief summary of the planned loan, borrower qualifications and compensating factors, and missing documentation.

Submit Loan Package

You will submit the loan package according to the preferences of the lender. Some underwriting teams will accept fax transmittals while others require that you mail a hard copy of the package to their offices. You should ensure that all submittals are sent in a timely manner.

Receive Loan Approval

After reviewing the loan file, underwriting will issue a decision. This decision can be denied, approved, or suspended.

- Denied means that the loan file does not meet the criteria for the loan program.

  The reason for the denial will be included with the denial notice.

  You should discuss the denial with the loan officer to determine if the reason for the denial can be corrected.

  > If the issue was a simple error and can be corrected, the loan officer will handle the remittal.

  > If the issue is one that cannot be corrected, you must issue a notice of denial to the borrower.

  You will save the file and all of the file contents in the location your office has designated for old loan file storage.

- If underwriting issues a suspension, they will provide you with details that define the reasons the file is suspended.

  A suspended file is missing some critical element that is necessary for underwriting to make a determination about the loan request.

  You should review the reason for the suspension with the loan officer, take the steps necessary to correct the file deficiency and then resubmit the package for review by underwriting.

- Each time you submit an initial loan package to the underwriting department, you are seeking an approval with stipulations.

  This stipulation list will become your primary focus over the coming days with regard to this loan file. You will gather the documentation items necessary to meet the stipulation list inclusions.

Upon receiving the notice that a file is approved with stipulations, you will inform the loan officer of the approval and stipulation requirements.

The loan officer will review the approval and confirm that the terms meet the parameters of the loan the borrower is expecting.

You will then proceed with the documentation and file processing requirements.

Documentation Requests	The first resource for obtaining missing documentation or file information is often the borrower. You should call the borrower with a list of the required stipulations. During the conversation, you will want to confirm the commitment terms of the file with the borrower to ensure that they have a full understanding of the loan and to solidify their commitment to your loan program.

You should also mail a list of the necessary stipulations, commitment letter, and welcome letter to the borrower.

If a real estate agent is involved in the transaction, you should send a copy of the commitment letter to the Real Estate Agent. If the borrower is not yet working with an agent, you should discuss the outbound referral with the loan officer. A part of the loan officer's job is to build referral and affinity relationships. Referring a borrower to a real estate agent is an excellent tool in building and solidifying the relationship your loan officer is building with that agent.

Documentation Orders (Borrower)

After all of the parties have been notified about the approval and stipulations necessary to close the loan; you will document the required details that relate to the borrower profile. For example, you will order a V. O. R. or V. O. M. to verify the status of the mortgage.

You should order any third party documentation requested on the stipulation list relating to the borrower to ensure that these items are available in the file to facilitate a speedy closing. You will order the property related stipulations after the borrower has chosen a home to purchase.

Each loan program will have different documentation requirements.

Receive sales agreement

When the borrower has located the home they wish to purchase and negotiated an agreement with the seller for that purchase, you will receive a copy of the sales agreement

You should provide the loan officer with the sales agreement. They will restructure deal as needed to conform to the terms in the sales agreement.

Examples of items that may need restructured within the loan documents after the sales agreement is finalized are

> Seller Concession

> Sales Price

> Source of Funds

Issue Additional Disclosures	Certain disclosures may need to be provided to the borrower again after the deal is restructured. You will need to review the signed notices and disclosures and obtain the borrowers signature on any missing items.
Revise GFE/TIL	The loan officer will revise the Good Faith Estimate and Truth in Lending to conform to the final financial details dictated by the sales agreement. Upon completion of the restructured loan package, you will need to disclose the Good Faith Estimate and the Truth in Lending to the borrowers a second time. These revised documents will contain actual numbers rather than 'to be decided' information. This re-disclosure enables the borrower to see the best estimate of closing costs based on an actual property agreement.
Obtain missing documentation	At this time it is imperative that any remaining stipulations requested from the borrower or from third parties be secured.
Documentation Orders (Property)	You will Order the Title Search, Appraisal, and Inspections where applicable.

The type of loan being obtained and the negotiations in the sales agreement will dictate the type of inspections you must order.

> Title Request Form
>
> Inspections (where applicable)
>
> Appraisal Request Form
>
> Other inspections or documents

You should ensure that you order all of the necessary paperwork, inspections, title work, and other documentation in a timely manner. Pay close attention to the section of the sales agreement that dictates the settlement date for the transaction.

Finalize Conditions	Once you have obtained all of the conditions listed on the stipulation list, you will submit the package to underwriting for a final review and approval.

You should stack this submission in the order the stipulations were requested on the stipulation list. In most cases, it is not a good idea to send each stipulation as it comes into the office. Most underwriting teams prefer that you submit all of the necessary stipulations in one packaged submittal. This enables them to have all of the necessary information to issue a loan approval. The exception is the appraisal.

You should submit the appraisal as soon as it is received as the appraisal might cause additional stipulations pertaining to the property to be added to the condition sheet.

You should also review each stipulation that you receive to ensure that it does not contain any detail or issue that will create a delay in obtaining the approval. For example, if you receive the borrower's tax returns from the previous year and note a large discrepancy in income, you will wish to discuss this issue with the loan officer so that the matter may be documented and addressed immediately.

Perform Pre-Close

Once underwriting has issued the final loan commitment and the closing is scheduled, you should contact the borrower to perform a pre-close discussion.

If possible, arrange a meeting for the loan officer to meet with the borrower.

The loan officer will review the final terms of the loan with the borrower during the meeting. If the interest rate is not yet locked, the loan officer will prepare a lock request for you to submit.

It is a good idea to be certain the borrower understands every term on their finalized loan commitment. This helps to avoid turmoil at closing because of miscommunication or memory issues.

Closing

Most loan officer will attend their closings. Following closing it is a good idea to send a post-close package and referral request. As part of our marketing program, we have a whole system of post-close fliers and referral requests to use.

We recommend you send each borrower and the agents involved in the transaction certain items. These could include Thank You cards, Customer Surveys, Realtor Surveys, and Gift Certificates towards closing cost discounts to be passed along to a future referral.

Chapter

6

FILE DOCUMENTATION

Your primary functions are to process borrower applications, obtain substantiating documentation proving all of the information on the loan application, and process the loan to a closing. To accomplish these tasks, you must gain a comprehensive understanding of the classification methodology applied to the various borrower situations by the mortgage industry.

Most borrowers are classified into two groups based upon the loan products for which they can qualify. These are

- A Paper, which is also called prime or conforming paper

- B/C Paper sometimes called sub-prime or non-conforming paper.

The fundamental difference between a conforming and a non-conforming loan is that the guidelines of a conforming loan are structured under the parameters established by Fannie Mae and Freddie Mac. Fanny Mae and Freddie Mac are the two of the largest entities that purchase mortgage loans from lenders to package into securities and sell to investors within the secondary mortgage market. Because these two entities are the largest purchasers of mortgage portfolios, the guidelines that they establish are considered the industry standard, with regard to borrower credit, income, down payment, debt ratio, and maximum loan amounts.

Any lending institution that intends to sell their packaged loans to an investor within the secondary mortgage market must consider these guidelines when providing mortgage funds to an applicant. If the application package does not meet the standards set forth by Fanny Mae and Freddie Mac, the likelihood of the lending institution being able to transfer the loan to an investor is diminished.

Within the category of conforming or conventional loans there is a sub-category termed Government Loans. Government loans sometimes enable a borrower whose situation or specifics falls outside of the standard conforming parameters to obtain a mortgage loan. Government loans are underwritten by the government and typically carry an insurance against default known as private mortgage insurance. This insurance enables borrowers whose credit, employment history, down payment amount, or other factors do not meet standard lending guidelines to obtain financing. These types of loans also carry very strict guidelines and parameters but the requirements are slightly lower in nature than those in the base conforming market.

The most common government loans are the F. H. A. and V.A. loans. Within these broad loan types are sub-types that offer different program specifics, approval parameters, and guidelines that will enable still more borrowers to qualify for mortgage financing.

The packages created by bundling groups of government underwritten loan products are typically sold through Ginnie Mae. Ginnie Mae purchases mortgage loans from lenders to package into securities and sell to investors within the secondary mortgage market. Ginnie Mae loans are the most popular type of mortgage-backed securities because they are guaranteed by the U.S. government and usually provide higher returns than investment opportunities outside of the mortgage offerings.

Non-conforming loans are loans with a different set of criteria than the guidelines set forth by Fannie Mae and Freddie Mac. This criterion still considers all of the aspects of a borrowers file such as credit history, employment history, down payment, and debt to income ratios but sets the minimum levels for each item at a lower level than the conforming parameters. The types of borrowers who seek non-conforming loans include individuals whose situation is different from what is considered the norm. An example of a commonly encountered, non-conforming profile would be the self-employed borrower. Guidelines also exist that enable individuals with poor credit histories to obtain mortgage financing but these guidelines will require higher costs and fees, down payment amount, and other matters than the conforming loan products.

The fact that the non-conforming loan is structured under a set of guidelines that will fall below those sought by investors interested in the Fannie Mae, Freddy Mac and Ginnie Mae loan portfolios does not mean that these loans are not commonly transferred on the secondary mortgage market. The non-conforming loan will carry a higher interest rate and more costs than the conforming loan. This higher rate helps to offset the increased investment risk associated with the lower guideline standards of the non-conforming loan. Investing pools seeking to purchase the non-conforming loan portfolios will be those who can bear a higher level of risk in exchange for potentially higher returns.

Each of these general programs will have various approval levels and loan products. Each of these specific programs will have slightly different borrower qualifications and documentation requirements. We have been illustrating the basis for the loan programs and the general documentation necessary throughout the coursework. You should become familiar with the specifics of each loan program your office uses to obtain funding for borrowers and gain an understanding of the documentation requirements of each program. In general, you will need to gain the documentation necessary to prove the creditworthiness of the borrower and the value of the property against which the loan is being issued. To do this, you will obtain documentation from many sources, compile all of the documentation into an understandable order, and remit all of the documentation to the underwriter assigned to the loan file.

After the initial meeting with the borrower, you will have a variety of documents to submit to the Underwriter. These are items such as the loan application, credit report, and all available substantiating documents provided by the borrower. The underwriter will review of the information and make sure that it conforms to the guidelines that the specific loan program requested has set forth. The underwriter will review the borrowers

- Income and Debt Ratios

- Employment History

- Credit History

- Savings / Source of Money for Down Payment

- The sales contract and the property appraisal if these are available at the time of the submittal.

Once the underwriter has reviewed the entire file, they will issue a written decision. This decision can take one of three forms.

Approved	meaning that everything in the file meets the guidelines for the loan program being requested.
Conditional	or suspended meaning that Additional documentation is needed to issue final determination on the file.
Denied	meaning that aspects of the file do not conform to the guidelines

If the loan is approved, the underwriter will provide you with a written loan approval that defines any additional item or documents that may need to be provided before the approval can be cleared for closing. These items are called "Conditions" or stipulations. A loan may be approved but still require updated "conditions" or items.

There are two types on conditions:

Prior to Loan Conditions   are items that must be provided and reviewed by the underwriter before the loan closing documents can be requested.

Prior to loan conditions must be given to the underwriter before the closing date can be scheduled.

Prior to Closing Conditions   are items that must be provided and reviewed by the underwriter or loan funder before the loan can close and funds for the closing can be released.

Prior to closing conditions can be provided to the underwriter at any time up to the time of the closing meeting.

The loan processing of the file is the most time consuming aspect of the loan process.

The true definition of loan processing is the preparation of the loan file for presentation to the underwriting department.

If the borrower did not provide all of the original documents necessary to process the file at the initial application meeting, the processing stage is the time you will request these items again.

The processing stage is comprised of gathering all of the documents necessary to substantiate the creditworthiness of the borrower, value, and condition of the property, and ability of the seller to transfer the title to the property free and clear of any blemishes.

Some of the file documents required by underwriting must be verified by what is considered an uninterested third party. These verifications require that you contact a resource besides the borrower, seller, or real estate agent to obtain proof that the information contained in the borrower application and loan file is correct. You will use the borrower consent form and the forms created for the specific entity to which you are requesting information to obtain a statement verifying the specific detail.

Each aspect of the loan file must be fully documented in compliance with the underwriting guidelines applicable to the specific loan program. Ensuring that the correct and complete documentation is included in the loan file is your job.

You must properly document every loan package you submit to the Underwriting Department. Without the ability to review all proper documentation necessary, the Underwriting team cannot make a valid decision on your loan package. If the documentation is incomplete or missing, the underwriting department will request additional items or stipulations.

STACKING THE FILE

The loan process is much smoother if you provide all necessary documentation at the time of submission rather than submitting documentation based on a stipulation lists. We have been reviewing applicable documentation requirements throughout the coursework.

Each time you submit a stipulation the Underwriter in charge of that particular loan must re-review the entire package. This is a time consuming and lengthy method of gaining approvals. Many times, additional items will be required to clarify the stipulations you have just submitted. Most important – sending packages in pieces is a very irritating practice that will not endear you to the underwriting team! By submitting packages piece meal, you create additional work for the underwriting team.

If you do not gather as many stipulations as possible at the initial application, you will gain a reputation of "stipping a loan to death". This reputation will cause referral partners and borrowers to doubt your professionalism and capabilities. It is also more time consuming to return to referral partners and borrowers for documentation necessary to close the loan.

Each time you submit a loan package there will be a transmittal summary or underwriting submission form your team prefers to have as a cover sheet. This sheet will usually contain a checklist of items the underwriting team requires to adequately review a loan package and make a decision for pre-approval. You will need to stack the items you are submitting in the order they appear on the submission form.

If there is no submission form, a best practice is to stack the items according to the usefulness and importance.

KENNEY

STACKING ORDER CHECKLIST

___ Loan Coversheet

___ Loan Submission Form

___ Stacking Order Checklist

___ Full 1008 or underwriting transmittal summary

___ Full, signed 1003 application

___ Purpose of Refinance Letter if applicable to the transaction

___ Credit Report

___ Credit Supplements if any are applicable to the loan file

___ Letter of explanation regarding any questionable or derogatory item on the credit report

___ A verification of mortgage or rent form or 12 months cancelled rent checks

___ All Bankruptcy Discharge Documentation if it is applicable to the transaction

___ A Divorce Decree if it is applicable to the transaction

___ A verification of deposit if checking or savings funds will be used toward the funds to close

___ A breakdown of the source of funds for closing

___ Gift letters signed by donors if they are applicable to the transaction

___ Verification of employment forms

___ Most Recent 30 Days Pay stubs

___ W-2's or full tax returns from preceding two years

___ Documentation of other income if it is applicable to the transaction

___ Sales Agreement including all pages and addendums

___ Rental or Lease Agreements if they are applicable to the transaction

___ Appraisal Report with original photographs

___ Preliminary Title Report

___ Title Commitment

___ Copy of any exiting note if the transaction is a refinance transaction

___ Escrow or funding instructions

___ Original Good Faith Estimate and Truth in Lending disclosures

___ ECOA, Fair Lending, and other Applicable Disclosures

___ Broker Agreements

___ And any other documentation specific to the loan file.

UNDERWRITING SUBMISSION FORM
FAX _____

Date: _____	*Broker Name:* _____
Broker Code: _____	Broker Contact: _____
Broker Phone: _____	Broker FAX: _____

If loan is locked – provide Loan Number: _____

Borrower's Name: _____

Co-Borrower's Name: _____

Purchase Price: $_____ LTV: _____% CLTV: _____%

Appraised Value: $_____ Loan Amount: $_____

LOAN PRODUCT	PURPOSE	OCCUPANCY	PROPERTY TYPE
__ 30 Yr Fixed	__ Purchase	__ Primary Residence	__ SFR
__ 15 Yr Fixed	__ Refi No Cash	__ Second Home	__ 2 Family
__ FHA/VA	__ Refi Cash out	__ Investment	__ 3-4 Family
__ FNMA Fallout			__ Condo/PUD
__ Lite Doc			
__ Other _____			

DOCUMENTATION
__ Signed 1003
__ Signed Good Faith
__ Pre-qualification 1003
__ Consent for Credit Check
__ Credit Report
__ VOR/VOM
__ W2/Tax Returns
__ Pay Stubs
__ Source of Funds
__ Other _____

_____

REQUEST INFORMATION: _____

_____

_____

_____

6:1 Sample Form – Underwriting Submission

KENNEY

Submission Sheet

DATE SUBMITTED: _____ ACCOUNT EXECUTIVE: _____
BROKER: _____
ADDRESS: _____
CONTACT: _____ PHONE: _____ FAX: _____

<table>
<tr><td colspan="4" align="center">BORROWER/LOAN INFORMATION</td></tr>
<tr><td colspan="2">BORROWER: _____</td><td colspan="2">SSN: _____</td></tr>
<tr><td colspan="2">CO-BORROWER: _____</td><td colspan="2">SSN: _____</td></tr>
<tr><td colspan="4">PROPERTY ADDRESS: _____</td></tr>
<tr><td>( ) Owner Occupied</td><td>( ) Purchase</td><td>( ) Full Doc</td><td>( ) SFR</td></tr>
<tr><td>( ) 2nd Home</td><td>( ) Refinance</td><td>( ) Lite Doc</td><td>( ) Townhouse</td></tr>
<tr><td>( ) Non-owner Occupied</td><td></td><td>( ) Stated Doc</td><td>( ) _____</td></tr>
<tr><td colspan="2">LOAN AMOUNT: $_____</td><td colspan="2">PROGRAM: _____</td></tr>
<tr><td colspan="2">APPRAISED VALUE: $_____</td><td colspan="2">RATE: _____ TERM: _____</td></tr>
<tr><td colspan="2">SALES PRICE: $ _____</td><td colspan="2">LTV: _____ CLTV: _____</td></tr>
</table>

BROKERS FEES

ORIGINATION _____%   _____

REBATE _____%   _____

PROCESSING   _____

APPRAISAL   _____

CREDIT REPORT   _____

_____   _____

_____   _____

<table>
<tr><td colspan="2" align="center">FILE STACKING ORDER</td></tr>
<tr><td>__ SUBMISSION FORM</td><td>__ VOE'S</td></tr>
<tr><td>__ TYPED 1008</td><td>__ CURRENT PAYSTUBS</td></tr>
<tr><td>__ TYPED 1003</td><td>__ LAST 2 YEARS W-2'S/1099'S</td></tr>
<tr><td>__ HANDWRITTEN 1003</td><td>__ YTD PROFIT & LOSS STMT (SELF-EMP)</td></tr>
<tr><td>__ PURPOSE LETTER</td><td>__ LAST 2 YEARS 1040'2</td></tr>
<tr><td>__ CREDIT EXPLANATION</td><td>__ LAST 2 YEARS 1120/1065</td></tr>
<tr><td>__ CREDIT REPORT</td><td>__ APPRAISAL WITH ORIGINAL PHOTOS</td></tr>
<tr><td>__ VOM/12 MONTH RENT CKS</td><td>__ PRELIMINAY TITLE</td></tr>
<tr><td>__ BK SCHEDULE & DIS</td><td>__ COPY OF EXISTING NOTE</td></tr>
<tr><td>__ DIVORCE DECREE</td><td>__ EXECUTED SALES CONTRACT</td></tr>
<tr><td>__ VOD</td><td>__ BROKERS DISCLOSURES</td></tr>
</table>

ORIGINAL PACKAGE REQUIRED

6:2 Sample Form – Submission Sheet

INCOME

A borrower must have adequate income to cover the repayment of their mortgage. Before a borrower can be approved for a loan, the stability of income and the probability of the continuance of that income must be shown. All of the income that will be used to qualify the borrower must be proven through acceptable sources including the borrower's employment record. Most loan programs will require that the employer confirm that the borrower will likely continue to be employed.

The stability of income is usually proven through the employment history.

> ➤ A two-year employment history is needed.

> ➤ It is preferable that the history is in the same line of work.

> ➤ The actual history can be comprised of multiple jobs if necessary.

> ➤ Education may be included as part of the 2 year history if it was education for the same profession.

You will gain information that details the two-year employment history when you complete the pre-qualification questionnaire. The borrower will inform you of the type of employment or income they will be using to qualify for the loan. You will obtain documentation that proves this history.

Salary or W-2 Income	You must obtain documentation that shows proof that a two-year history of receiving this income exists and proof that this income is likely to continue.
	The two-year history can be established by including the most recent 30-days pay stubs and the year-end Ww-2 for the prior two years.
	Continuance of employment will be established using a V. O. E. form.
Overtime or Bonus Income	The borrower must show proof that a two-year history of receiving this income exists.
	They must also show proof that this income is likely to continue.
	The borrower will need to provide documentation, such as pay stubs for the most recent 30-day period of the present year and the final W-2 for the prior 2 years.

*	Each of these documents must show the inclusion of the overtime or bonus income.

The income will be factored as an average over the previous two years.

You will need to obtain a V. O. E. from the employer confirming the history and future probability of continuance for this income.

Part-time Income

If the borrower will use part-time income, such as income from a second job or seasonal employment, a two-year history of receiving this income must also be proven.

The documentation must show that the borrower has a 2-year history of receiving this income without interruption

The V. O. E. will be used to show proof that the part-time income has a high probability of continuing

If the income cannot be used as qualifying income because of an interruption in receipt of the income, a lack of a two-year history or the inability to confirm the likelihood of the continuance of this income, you will still wish to document it. It may be considered as a compensating factor.

Commission Income

Commission income is based on the average of the previous 2 years income.

The borrower must provide their full Federal Tax Returns, including all schedules, covering the past two years and you must obtain a year to date income statement from the employer.

Any un-reimbursed business expenses must be subtracted from the gross income in order to gain the usable income figures.

Retirement, Social Security Income, Public Assistance, or Disability Income

If the borrower is using retirement or social security income as part of their qualification package, verification from the source of the income must be obtained.

An award letter from the social security administration or a statement of retirement income will be used for documentation purposes.

If the income will discontinue within 3 years, the income cannot be used to qualify the borrower and used only as a compensating factor.

Alimony, Child Support, or
Income from Separate Maintenance

This income is not required for qualification, but a borrower may choose to use this income if they wish.

To use this income, the borrower will need to supply a 12-month payment history from the ex-spouse or the courts showing timely payment will be required.

Evidence that such payment will continue for at least 3 years must be provided.

A copy of the

- divorce decree

- settlement agreement

- other legal documents illustrating

  ➢   amount of the income

  ➢   history of the income

  ➢   term for the continuance of this income

will be necessary.

Notes Receivable

In order to use income from a note, the borrower must provide a copy of the endorsed and binding note.

The borrower must also provide proof that payments have been received for a minimum of 12 months.

*   This proof can be in the form of bank statements or copies of the cancelled payment checks.

If the note expires within 3 years, it cannot be used for qualifying but may be considered as a compensating factor.

Interest and Dividends	Interest and dividend income may be used if documentation, such as tax returns or account statements, illustrates a 2-year history or receiving this income.
Rental Income	Rent received from investment properties owned by the borrower may be used if the receipt of these rents can be documented.
	Income from roommates and boarders is not acceptable.
	Rental income is calculated from the borrower's Schedule E of the 10 40.
	Depreciation can be added back in to the total received.
	You should note that while positive rental income is considered as gross income, negative rental income must be treated as a recurring liability.
	Copies of the leases must be provided to prove this income.
Self-Employment Income	A borrower with 25% or more ownership interest in a business can be considered self-employed.
	A borrower must have more than a one-year history for income to be considered.
	A two-year full tax return will be required.
Bank Statements	Some loan programs will allow the borrower to use the deposits shown on 12-months or 24-months bank must be sent statements as proof of income.
	In order to qualify for a bank statement program, the borrower's position must validate the probability that their business is cash based business.
	The deposits showing on 12 consecutive months' bank statements will be totaled and divided by the 12 months to arrive at an average income.

Keep in mind that this is considered a light documentation loan and may be penalized with higher interest rates or a higher down payment requirement.

THIRD PARTY VERIFICATION

Many factors of the loan require verification of information. This verification must be obtained from a third party who has access to specific details concerning a borrower's profile.

It is important to understand a borrower's right to financial privacy. Details concerning Financial Privacy and Authorization to Release/Obtain Information forms in are included in ethics and disclosure chapter. If you are unsure of the process and requirements for the completion of these forms, you will need to review the pertinent section of Chapter for additional information.

The following pages provide you with example forms for specific situations.

- Verification of Employment (VOE)

- Verification of Deposit (VOD)

- Verification of Rent (VOR)

- Verification of Mortgage (VOM)

Each of these verification forms will provide specific information concerning your borrower's situation, past, present and future.

You should forward these verification forms to the appropriate company or agency for completion. The forms should be accompanied by a copy of the borrowers consent to release information.

VERIFICATION OF EMPLOYMENT (VOE)

In addition to verifying the income of the borrower through acceptable documentation, underwriting will often require verification of the borrower's employment and the probability of continued employment before the closing of the loan.

Verification forms must be sent to the employer to confirm all vital facts regarding employment, income, and continued employment.

A **Verification of Employment (VOE)** is a form sent to past and present employers for last two years to verify income and time on the job. Some employers have an automated 900 number for employment verification.

Receiving a verification of employment typically takes 1 to 2 weeks so you will wish to send your request early in the loan process.

You will complete sections 1 through 7 of the VOE request form.

➢ You will include the name of the employer and the applicable supervisor from whom the information is being requested.

➢ You should enter both your name and the company name as confirmation to the employer regarding the source of the request.

➢ Your full mailing address and any fax number that may be used for the return of the V. O. E. form should be included in the heading.

➢ You will sign the form as verification of the source of the request.

➢ Include your title and the date of the request.

➢ Section 7 allows you to include the information pertaining to the applicant so the employer has an easy reference when completing the form.

➢ The applicant should sign the form so that the employer knows that the release of the applicable employment data is authorized by the borrower.

* You may also attach the credit and information consent form that the borrower completed during the application process as additional verification that the borrower authorizes the release of the employment data.

The employer will complete PART 2 of the form and return it to your office.

When you receive the completed V. O. E., you should review all of the inclusions to ensure that they match the information contained within the borrower application.

If there is any discrepancy between the income information, employment data, or other inclusions of the forms, you should address this discrepancy and ensure that the incorrect information is corrected before submitting the verifications to underwriting for review.

Mortgage Lending – Home Mortgage Loan Processing

REQUEST FOR VERIFICATION OF EMPLOYMENT

Privacy Act Notice: This information is to be used by the agency collecting it or its assignees in determining whether you qualify as a prospective mortgagor under its program. It will not be disclosed outside the agency except as required and permitted by law. You do not have to provide this information, but if you do not your application for approval as a prospective mortgagor or borrower may be delayed or rejected. The information requested in this form is authorized by Title 38, USC. Chapter 37 (if VA); by 12 USC, Section 1701 et. Seq (if HUD/FHA); by 42 USC, Section 1452b (if HUD/CPD); and Title 42 USC, 1471 et. Seq., or 7 USC. 1971 et. Deq. (if USDA/FmHA).

Instructions   Lender – Complete items 1 through 7. Have applicant complete item 8. Forward directly to employer named in item 1.
                 Employer – Please complete either Part II or Part III as applicable. Complete Part IV and return directly to lender named in item 2.
                 This form is to be transmitted directly to the lender and is not to be transmitted through the applicant or any other party.

Part I – Request

1. To (Name and address of employer)	2. From (Name and address of Lender)

I certify that this verification has been sent directly to the employer and ahs not passed through the hands of the applicant or any other interested party.

2. Signature of Lender	4. Title	4. Date	6. Lender's Number (Optional)

I have applied for a mortgage loan and stated that I am now or was formerly employed by you. My signature below authorizes verification of this information.

7. Name and Address of Applicant (include employee or badge number)	8. Signature of Applicant

Part II – Verification of Present Employment

9. Applicant's Date of Employment	10. Present Position	11. Probability of Continued Employment

12A. Current Gross Base Pay (enter Amount and Check Period) __ Annual __ Hourly __ Monthly __ Other (specify) $ _____ __ Weekly	13 For Military Personnel Only		14. If Overtime or Bonus is Applicable Is Its Continuance Likely? Overtime __ Yes __ No Bonus __ Yes __ No 15. If paid hourly – average hours per week

			Pay Grade	

Type	Year to Date	Past Year 20_	Past Year 20_			
				Type	Monthly Amount	
				Base Pay	$	
Base Pay	$	$	$	Rations	$	16. Date of applicant's next pay increase
Overtime	$	$	$	Flight or Hazard	$	17. Projected amount of next pay increase
				Clothing	$	
Commissions	$	$	$	Quarters	$	18. Date of applicant's last pay increase
				Pro Pay	$	
Bonus	$	$	$	Overseas or Combat	$	19. Amount of last pay increase
Total	$	$	$	Variable Housing Allowance	$	

20. Remarks (If employee was off work for any length of time, please indicate time period and reason)

Part III Verification of Previous Employment

21. Date Hired	23. Salary/Wage at Termination Per (Year) (Month) (Week)
22. Date Terminated	Base _____ Overtime _____ Commissions _____ Bonus _____
24. Reason for Leaving	25. Position Held

Part IV – Authorized Signature – Federal statutes provide severe penalties for any fraud, intentional misrepresentation, or criminal connivance or conspiracy purposed to influence the issuance of any guaranty or insurance by the VA Secretary, the U.S.D.A., FmHA/FHA Commissioner, or the HUD/CPD Assistant Secretary.

26. Signature of Employer	27. Title (please print or type)	28. Date
29. Print or type named signed in item 26	30. Phone No.	

6:3 Sample Form – Verification of Employment – HUD Release

MORTGAGE OR RENTAL HISTORY

The verification of mortgage or rental history is used to verify the payment history of the borrower relating to their previous housing obligations.

Mortgage or rental history is often used to project the probability of a borrower repaying their new mortgage in a timely manner. The theory behind this is that the manner that the borrower paid previous housing obligations reflects the seriousness with which they will approach the new housing payment obligations.

Mortgage histories are frequently included in a credit report.

If the mortgage or rental history is not included in the credit report, it must be verified in another manner.

> V. O. M. stands for Verification of Mortgage

> V. O. R. stands for Verification of Rent

These Verification forms are sent to a mortgage holder or a rental management company to verify the history of an account.

> ➢ Many lenders will not accept verification forms from a private party as these can easily be falsified. In that instance, you will need to acquire alternate documentation.
>
> The borrower may supply copies of the most recent 12 months cancelled housing payment checks or money orders.
>
> If these are not available,
>
> The most recent 12 months bank statements can be obtained from either the borrower or the landlord showing 12 months concurrent withdrawals or deposits for the monthly housing payments.

More and more lenders are placing equal or greater weights on verification of rent or mortgages payments as on credit scores. It is a common belief that the history of payment of a mortgage or rent in the borrowers past reflects the probable payment performance in the borrower's future.

REQUEST FOR VERIFICATION OF RENT OR MORTGAGE

Privacy Act Notice: This information is to be used by the agency collecting it or its assignees in determining whether you qualify as a prospective mortgagor under its program. It will not be disclosed outside the agency except as required and permitted by law. You do not have to provide this information, but if you do not your application for approval as a prospective mortgagor or borrower may be delayed or rejected. The information requested in this form is authorized by Title 38, USC. Chapter 37 (if VA); by 12 USC, Section 1701 et. Seq (if HUD/FHA); by 42 USC, Section 1452b (if HUD/CPD); and Title 42 USC, 1471 et. Seq., or 7 USC. 1971 et. Deq. (if USDA/FmHA).

Instructions	Lender – Complete items 1 through 8. Have applicant complete item 9. Forward directly to landlord named in item 1. Landlord Creditor – Please complete Items 10 through 18 and return directly to lender named in item 2. This form is to be transmitted directly to the lender and is not to be transmitted through the applicant or any other party.

Part I – Request

1. To (Name and address of Landlord Creditor)	2. From (Name and address of Lender)

I certify that this verification has been sent directly to the landlord/creditor and ahs not passed through the hands of the applicant or any other interested party.

2. Signature of Lender	4. Title	4. Date	6. Lender's Number (Optional)

7. Information To Be Verified

Property Address	Account in the Name of	Account Number
	__ Mortgage __ Rental __ Land Contract	

I have applied for a mortgage loan. My signature below authorizes verification of mortgage or rent information.

8. Name and Address of Applicant(s)	9. Signature of Applicant(s) X X

Part II – To Be Completed by the Landlord/Creditor

We have received an application for a loan from the above, to whom we understand you rent or have extended a loan. In addition to the information requested below, please furnish us with any information you might have that will assist us in processing the loan.

__ Rental Account	__ Mortgage Account	__ Land Contract
10. Tenant Rented from _____ to _____ Amount of rent $_____ per _____ Number of late payments _____ Is account satisfactory? __ Yes __ No	11. Date account opened _____ Original contract amount $_____ Current account balance $_____ Monthly Payment (P&I) $_____ Payment with T&I $_____ Is account current? __ Yes __ No Was loan assumed? __ Yes __ No Satisfactory account? __ Yes __ No	12. Interest Rate _____ % __ Fixed __ ARM __ FHA __ VA __ CONV __ Other Next pay date _____ No. of late payments _____ No. of late charges _____ Owner of First Mortgage _____

Payment History for the previous 12 months must be provided n order to comply with secondary mortgage market requirements.

13. Additional information which may be of assistance in determination of credit worthiness

14. Signature of Landlord/Creditor Representative	15. Title (please print or type)	Date

17. Please print or type name signed in Item 14

6:4 Sample Form – Verification of Rent or Mortgage – HUD Release

The completion of the verification of rent or mortgage form is similar to the completion and remittal of the verification of employment.

➤ You will again enter the applicable information into section 1 and 2 of the form.

➤ You should sign and date the form and include your title to illustrate to the mortgage holder or landlord that you are an authorized representative of the lending institution and therefore privy to this data.

➤ You will enter the borrowers PRESENT or PAST housing address into the field property address.

*   The address entered should be the one whose payment history you are verifying, not necessarily the borrower's present address. You should have the borrower sign the authorization so that the individual knows that they have approved the release of their personal history.

➤ The landlord or mortgage holder will complete part two of the form and return it to your office.

➤ Upon receipt of the completed document, you should verify that the payment history, payment amount, and term of occupancy equate to the information entered into the ten oh three.

*   If there is any discrepancy between the information contained on the form and the information in the borrowers file, you should have the incorrect forms corrected before submitting the file to underwriting for review.

SOURCE OF FUNDS

You will need to verify the source of the funds that the borrower will use for the transaction. Oftentimes, the source of funds will actually be a combination of sources used to arrive at the total figure that the borrower will use to total the amount of money needed to pay the down payment, closing costs, and other costs associated with the transaction.

➤ Each approval will come with a Loan to Value shortened as L. T. V.

The LTV is the amount the lender is willing to finance as opposed to the overall cost of the property.

➤ Some loans will come with a C. L. T. V. meaning Combined Loan to Value.

The combined loan to value is the additional amount the borrower may finance through subordinate financing with the seller of the property or an outside lending   source.

➤ The balance between the LTV or CLTV and the total price of the property including the sales price and all closings costs, must be sourced, often as the borrowers own funds.

Borrowers are often required to invest their own funds in the property to aid in securing the loan against default. Generally, the higher the credit risks the higher the percent of the borrowers required investment. The premise behind this requirement is that a borrower is less likely to default on a loan if they are losing their own personal funds through the default.

The borrower's cash investment in the property must be equal to the difference between the amount of the mortgage, excluding any up front fees, and the total costs to acquire the property. All funds must be verified through acceptable methods.

Savings and Checking

Some lending guidelines will require that the borrower have saved funds to close in a savings or checking account while others will accept that the borrower has saved the funds for close in cash.

* You will want to confirm the specific holding requirements of the loan program you will be documenting.

Seasoning

Those lending programs that require the funds be kept in a savings or checking account may also require that the funds be seasoned.

The premise behind requiring seasoning of funds is that the time necessary to season funds helps to prove that the funds are the borrowers own money and not a result of a loan or gift from another entity or individual.

Seasoning means that the funds have been in the borrowers account a specific length of time. Often 90 days.

To prove seasoned funds, you will obtain a bank statement or a verification of deposit that covers the required seasoned term.

Certain loan programs do not require seasoned funds. These are often non-conventional programs.

> The underwriter will review the bank statements or verification of deposit form to insure that the funds have been in the borrower's possession for the required length of time.

> The underwriter will also use these statements to determine if the borrower is balancing and managing their bills properly.

> You will wish to review the bank statements before remittal.

> If the bank statement contains non-sufficient funds notations, the underwriter will require an explanation for the poor financial management and may place a hold on the approval.

> The underwriter may also use the bank statements to ensure that the debts illustrated on the credit report match up to the monthly payments shown on the statement.

> They will review the deposits showing on the statements to determine if they are close to what the borrower is netting on their paycheck.

➢ If there are any large deposits, recurring debt not illustrated in the borrowers debt listing or other unusual entry on the bank statement, they will need to be explained.

* An occasional "N. S. F." may be cleared by underwriting if there is proper explanation as to why it occurred.

Cash saved at home

A borrower who has saved their money saved at home, can still purchase a home using this money.

The borrower must provide a written explanation of how the money was saved and the length of time taken to do so.

The lender will review the explanation to determine the creditability of these savings.

They will compare the statements to the borrowers

➢ Income

➢ Spending Habits

➢ History of using Financial Institutions for savings purposes

Many loan programs have limitations on the amount of cash saved at home, also termed mattress money that may be used for a transaction.

You will wish to check the specific underwriting guidelines for the specific program before allocating this mattress money to the transaction.

➢ If the amount of mattress money exceeds the limitations of the loan program, an alternate source of funds may be needed to gain underwriting approval for the transaction.

➢ If an alternate source of funds is not available, the funds may need to be deposited into a financial institution and the transaction placed on hold until the seasoning term requirements have been met.

The underwriter may request additional documentation relating to a mattress money transaction, including

- additional bank statements

- borrower statements

- details regarding non-debt to income related expenses

- other documentation specific to the situation

Gift Funds

Many loan programs will allow a homebuyer to receive all or some of the down payment for the purchase of a home as a "Gift".

A gift means that the borrower does not have to pay the funds received back. There are many acceptable sources of gift funds including.

➢ a relative

➢ the borrower's employer or labor union

➢ a charitable organization

➢ a governmental agency or public entity that has a program or established to provide homeownership assistance to low and moderate income families

NO REPAYMENT OF THIS GIFT MAY BE EXPECTED OR IMPLIED.

To use gift funds for the purchase a gift letter must be submitted to Underwriting.

This letter must be signed by both parties and state that there is no requirement to repay the funds received.

The gift letter must specify

- the dollar amount given

- be signed by the donor and the borrower

- state that no repayment is required

- o show the donor's name, address, telephone number, and relationship to the borrower

- o It must also contain language asserting that the funds given to the homebuyer were not made available to the donor from any person or entity with an interest in the sale of the property including the seller, real estate agent, broker, builder, loan processor, or any entity associated with any of these individuals or entities.

If the gift funds are already in the homebuyer's account

- o You must document the transfer of the funds from the donor to the homebuyer by obtaining a copy of the canceled check or other withdrawal document showing that the withdrawal is from the donor's personal account along with the homebuyer's deposit slip or bank statement that shows the deposit.

If the gift funds are to be provided at closing
by certified check, the check must be from the donors account.

- o You must obtain a bank statement showing the withdrawal from the donor's personal account as well as a copy of the certified check.

If the donor purchased a cashier's check, money order, official check or any other type of bank check as a means of transferring the gift funds, then the donor must provide a withdrawal document or canceled check for the gift showing the funds came from the donor's personal account.

If the donor borrowed the gift funds and, thus, cannot provide the documentation from his or her bank or other savings account, the donor must provide evidence that those funds were borrowed from an acceptable source.

- o The donor cannot borrow the funds from a party to the transaction including the mortgage lender.

- o "Cash on hand" is often not an acceptable source of the donor's gift funds.

- o Example: A retirement account would be an acceptable source of gift funds.

There may be limitations on the amount of closing funds that may be received as a gift.

You will want to check the specific guidelines for the loan program to confirm the gift fund limits and ensure that the source of funds necessary does not exceed these limits.

If the money that the borrower needs exceeds the gift fund maximum limits, you will need to assist the borrower in sourcing the necessary money from one of the approved source of funds items on the list.

Gift Equity

If the sale of a property is between immediate relatives, gift equity may be given as a seller concession toward the overall cost of the loan.

- o Gift Equity is simply a reduction in the dollar amount the seller of the property expects to receive from the sale of the property.

- o The reduction is given in the form of equity rather than a monetary gift or a subordinate loan.

The amount of equity that can be given as a gift between relatives is subject to maximum limitations and you will need to review the underwriting guidelines for the particular loan program to determine this maximum.

Gift Equity can only be given between immediate relative.

Earnest Money Deposit

Upon making an offer on a property, most Real Estate Agents require the buyer to remit an Earnest Money Deposit.

This deposit protects the agency and the seller in the event the buyer's change their minds and cancels the deal.

- o Once an offer has been accepted, the property is removed from the market.

- o If the buyer backs out of a deal once the property has been removed from the market, the earnest money deposit is retained between the sellers and the real estate agent.

- o These funds are used as payment for the loss of time involved and any costs incurred.

If the transaction progresses as expected, the earnest money deposit is held in escrow, typically by the real estate agent and is used towards the borrower's funds necessary to close the deal.

In most cases, the source of the earnest money deposit will not need to be confirmed.

- If the amount of earnest money exceeds 2% of the sales price or appears to be excessive based on the borrower's history of accumulating savings, the deposit amount, and the source of funds may require verification.

Otherwise, satisfactory documentation includes a copy of the borrower's cancelled check or verification from the bank.

Seller Concession

Most loan programs allow the seller to allocate a portion of their funds toward the payment of the borrower's non-recurring closing costs and possibly towards the borrower's necessary pre-paids.

- This amount is vary by loan program but typically ranges from 3 to 6 percent of the sale price of the property.

Seller's concessions must be agreed upon in the Sales Agreement to count as source of funds.

You will document the seller concession by remitting the sales agreement to the underwriter.

You should also confirm that the seller concessions are allocated on the HUD 1 in the correct location.

Example: Some loan programs will not allow seller concession toward recurring closing costs and the closing department will reject the closing documents if the HUD 1 illustrates that the seller concession is being used to pay these bills.

Prepaid Charges

Any cost involved with the loan that the borrower has paid in advance of closing can be considered funds to close the loan.

Example: Many borrowers will pay the appraisal fee, application fee, or credit report fee at some time during the loan process.

You will document these payments through copies of the bill and corresponding checks.

These amounts may then be allocated as a source of funds to close the loan.

Prepaid charges will need to be documented in the form a copy of the check written to the lender or service provider.

401K or Retirement: Borrowers may draw or borrow from a 401K or Retirement Account and use the funds received toward the closing.

- o If the borrower must borrow against an account, they must be able to qualify with the monthly repayment amount resulting from this advance.

- o You will need to obtain a statement illustrating the monthly repayment amount required on the loan from the account.

- o This amount must be factored as a recurring liability and the borrower must be able to meet the debt to income qualification requirements of the program.

Sales Proceeds The sale of an asset is considered an acceptable source of funds for most programs.

The borrower must provide adequate documentation of the value of the item sold, the amount received from the sale, and proof that the sale occurred.

Documentation may include

- o a copy of the bill of sale or the HUD-1 Settlement Statement if the property sold was real estate

- o a copy of the check or verification of transfer of funds for the buyer to the borrower

- o a copy of the borrower's deposit slip or bank statement showing the deposit of the funds

In some cases when the value of an item is in question, the borrower may need to prove that the sale price of the property was fair market value. This may be accomplished using appraisals, market condition proof, or other source of proof of value.

Rent Credit and
Option Premium

At times, you may be working on a transaction where the buyer has agreed to purchase the property from the seller under another transaction known as the lease option.

Under a lease option agreement, the buyer will typically give the seller a specific amount of money at the beginning of the transaction.

o   This money is termed an option payment.

It is similar to a down payment or earnest money deposit in that it is money credited by the seller to the buyer in the event the buyer chooses to purchase the property.

In exchange for the option premium, the seller agrees to sell the property to the buyer on or before a certain future date, at an agreed upon sum of money.

The buyer will occupy the property as a tenant until the purchase date.

If the buyer does not follow through with the purchase of the property, the seller retains the option premium in consideration of their removing the property from the sales market and holding any sale in abeyance for the buyer.

If the buyer follows through with the agreed upon purchase, the option premium is credited toward the purchase price and may be used as a source of funds.

o   You will document this source by remitting a copy of the original agreement between the buyer and the seller along with a copy of the check used to make the option payment.

Some lenders have set limitations on the amount of option payment that may be used toward a purchase.

If the option payment exceeds the limitations set by underwriting, a new agreement may be required that lowers the purchase price to enable a credit to the borrower for the excess amount paid.

o   Under a lease option, many sellers will agree to credit a portion of the borrower's current rental payment toward the purchase of the property the borrower.

The sellers will typically charge an amount for the monthly payment that is in excess of the fair market rent for similar property in the area.

This excess amount is typically considered an allowable source of funds for the purchase

o The borrower will need to provide a copy of the rental/lease agreement showing the option to purchase with the clause stating how much of the rental payment is to be used toward the purchase.

o You may also need to show proof that the rent payment is above the estimated fair market rent for other, similar properties in the area.

Fair market rent may be established by illustrating the rental income from similar rental properties of similar size and similar locations in the area.

o Underwriting will often allow only those portions of the rental payment that exceed the fair market rent for the area to be credited as a source of funds for close regardless of the agreement between the buyer and the seller..

Example   If the borrower has rented a home with a fair market rent of $750 a month the borrower may only use monies from payments that total above $750 per month.

If the borrower pays $1,000 a month, then $250 of each payment may be credited toward down payment funds.

If the borrower pays only $750 a month for this property then it is likely underwriting will allow none of the payment amount to be credited as down payment.

These are the most common source of funds acceptable to most Underwriting Teams. There are as many possibilities available as there will be borrowers in your office. Each situation is different and it is up to you to use your creativity in aiding your borrower in the sourcing of funds to close the loan.

Remember, any time you have a questionable source, run it past your Underwriting Team. They may have a method of documentation they will be willing to accept to consider this source as borrower funds toward closing.

Many of the sources of funds illustrated will require additional verification for documentation purposes. Some of this verification may be obtained from the borrower. Other verification documentation must be obtained from a third party source. The most common third party verification you will encounter is the Verifications of Deposit

The Verification of Deposit is a form sent to the borrower's banking institutions to verify average bank account balances for past 3 months.

Some banks will charge borrower a fee of up to $20 for this verification.

REQUEST FOR VERIFICATION OF DEPOSIT

Privacy Act Notice: This information is to be used by the agency collecting it or its assignees in determining whether you qualify as a prospective mortgagor under its program. It will not be disclosed outside the agency except as required and permitted by law. You do not have to provide this information, but if you do not your application for approval as a prospective mortgagor or borrower may be delayed or rejected. The information requested in this form is authorized by Title 38, USC, Chapter 37 (if VA); by 12 USC, Section 1701 et. Seq (if HUD/FHA); by 42 USC, Section 1452b (if HUD/CPD); and Title 42 USC, 1471 et. Seq., or 7 USC. 1971 et. Deq. (if USDA/FmHA).

Instructions Lender – Complete items 1 through 8. Have applicant complete item 9. Forward directly to depository named in item 1.
Depository – Please complete Items 10 through 18 and return DIRECTLY to lender named in item 2.
This form is to be transmitted directly to the lender and is not to be transmitted through the applicant or any other party.

PART I - REQUEST

1. To (Name and address of depository)	2. From (Name and address of Lender)

I certify that this verification has been sent directly to the bank or depository and ahs not passed through the hands of the applicant or any other interested party.

2. Signature of Lender	4. Title	4. Date	6. Lender's Number (Optional)

7. Information To Be Verified

Type of Account	Account in Name of	Account Number	Balance
			$
			$
			$

To Depository: I/We have applied for a mortgage loan and stated in my financial statement that the balance on deposit with you is as shown above. You are authorized to verify this information and to supply the lender identified above with the information requested in Items 10 through 13. Your response is solely a matter of courtesy for which no responsibility is attached to your institution or any of your officers.

8. Name and Address of Applicant(s)	9. Signature of Applicant(s)

PART II – VERIFICATION OF DEPOSITORY To Be Completed By Depository

10. Deposit Accounts of Applicant(s)

Type of Account	Account in Name of	Account Number	Balance
			$
			$
			$

11. Loans Outstanding To Applicants

Loan Number	Date of Loan	Original Amount	Current Balance	Installments (Monthly/Quarterly)		Secured By	Number of Late Payments
		$	$	$	per		
		$	$	$	per		
		$	$	$	per		

12. Please include any additional information which may be of assistance in determination of credit worthiness. (Please include information on loans paid-in-full in Item 11 above)

13. If the name(s) on the account(s) differ from those listed in Item 7, please supply the name(s) on the account(s) as reflected by your records.

PART III – Authorized Signature – Federal statutes provide severe penalty for any fraud, intentional misrepresentation, or criminal connivance or conspiracy purposed to influence the issuance of any guaranty or insurance by the VA Secretary, the U.S.D.A., FmHA/FHA Commissioner, or the HUD/CPD Assistant Secretary.

14. Signature of Depository Representative	15. Title (please print or type)	16. Date
17. Please print or type name signed in item 14	18. Phone No.	

6:5 Sample Form – Verification of Deposit – HUD Release

Credit Report

You will order a preliminary credit report when the initial application is completed.

You may be required to order an updated credit report if the loan process takes longer than underwriting allocates for a credit report.

- o Underwriting will set the standards for the age of the report.

- o It is important to meet or exceed these standards and to caution the borrower not to take any action that may alter the credit report during the loan process.

- o Any changes in the borrower's credit profile may create issues or changes to the loan approval status, causing delays in the closing of the loan.

Some underwriting teams require what is known as a tri-merge credit report or a full-factual credit report.

- o A tri-merge report is one that uses the data from all three major credit report bureaus and blends it onto a single report.

- o If the underwriting requests a full factual credit report, the credit bureau will verify all of the accounts and balances on the report prior to issuing the report to your office.

    A full factual report typically takes 2 - 5 business days for completion.

Credit Supplements

You may need to acquire additional supplements regarding specific credit issues.

These supplements can be obtained from the credit bureau by completing and submitting the request.

Request forms can typically be found on the last page of the credit report.

These credit supplements will serve to verify or clarify a specific matter found on the credit report and can usually be obtained within 2 to 5 business days of the request.

Purchase Contract, Addendums, Counter Offers	You will need to obtain a copy of the Purchase Contract, Addendums to the Sales Agreement and documentation related to counter offers for purchase transactions.
	These are the original contracts regarding the terms of the purchase of the property.
	All of the completed and signed forms will be needed for the loan file.
	You should obtain these forms before ordering the appraisal, as appraiser requires a copy of the contract to complete their functions.
	The realtor estate agent will typically provide these documents to you as soon as an agreement has been reached between the buyer and the seller. T
	The negotiation process between the buyer and seller typically takes between 2 and 10 days but may take longer depending on the complexity of the transaction.
Explanation Letters	You may need to obtain Letters of Explanation from the borrower.
	A letter of explanation is a letter written and signed by the borrower that explains any issues on the credit report, work history, bank account deposits, source of funds discrepancy, or other unusual matters relating to the file.
Appraisal	The Appraisal will be ordered from an underwriting approved appraiser. The appraiser will

- o go to the property

- o measure square footage

- o verify required conditions

- o check other recent comparable home sales

- o determine value of the home

You will need to verify that the appraiser you choose to complete the appraisal process is one that is approved by underwriting.

You may also wish to discuss the appraiser you will use with the loan officer, as an appraiser is an affinity service provider who sometimes works with potential inbound referrals.

- o The loan officer may wish to build a better referral relationship with a specific appraiser.

Appraisals usually take 1 week to complete but may take longer depending on your market.

- o You will wish to request a timeline from the appraiser.

- o You must ensure that the seller or real estate agent is aware that the appraisal has been ordered so that they can make themselves available to provide the appraiser with entry into the property. .

When you request the completion of the appraisal, you should provide the appraiser with all of the details and documentation that they will need to speed their activity.

- o The appraiser can obtain this information from other sources, but you have it available and ensuring that the necessary details and documents are in the hands of the appraiser immediately upon receipt of the request helps to build stronger affinity service relationships and assists in speeding the appraisal completion time aiding you in processing faster closings.

You should fill in the appraisal request form completely.

- o The branch or appraiser may have a different form that they prefer using for the request.

- o We have included a sample form to assist you in gaining an understanding of the actions that you must take when ordering an appraisal.

- o You may use this form if your branch or appraiser does not have a preferred form available for your use.

Appraisal Request Form

DATE: _____   FROM: _____
TO: _____   FAX: _____

PURCHASE/REFINANCE/OTHER   FHA/VA/RURAL HOUSING/CONVENTIONAL

APPLICANT/BORROWERS: _____ PHONE: _____

REAL ESTATE AGENT: _____ PHONE: _____

CONTACT INFORMATION: _____

PROPERTY INFORMATION: _____

ESTIMATED VALUE   _____   SALES PRICE: _____

LENDER'S NAME: _____

PAYMENT OPTION: _____

ADDITIONAL COMMENTS: _____

ITEMS ATTACHED: ___ Sales Agreement Page 1
                           ___ Sales Agreement Page 2
                           ___ Original Purchase Document
                           ___ Previous Appraisal
                           ___ Other: _____

6:6 Sample Form – Appraisal Request Form

1. You should include all of the contact information that the appraiser may need including the telephone numbers for the individuals the appraiser may need to contact.

   These include the real estate agent, the seller, and the closing company.

2. You should send the appropriate pages of a Sales Agreement.

   The appraiser will need to see the details included within page one of the sales agreement, and any addendums that relate to additional inclusions incorporated into the transfer.

   You should note in the comments section of the appraisal request that page one of the sales agreement is attached.

3. If you remit the appraisal request by fax, you should place the confirmation page that shows the date and time that the request was sent in the file.

If you remit the appraisal request by mail or in person, you should include a copy of the dated request cover sheet in the file so that you have documentation of the actions taken on the file.

4. You should always note exactly how the appraisal bill is to be paid under the Bill Payment field of the request form. Common choices include

> "Collect from Customer at door"
> "Bill Office"
> "Bill Customer"
> "At closing"

You should remember that the ordering loan office is ultimately responsible for the payment of the appraisal bill. If the appraiser does not obtain the payment via another method, the appraiser sends the bill to your office. This is the reason that many lenders now require the appraisal fees to be paid in advance.

5. You should log the request date on the file tracking form.

Seventy-two hours after you have sent the request, you should contact the appraiser to determine the status of the appraisal.

   o   If any issue exists that is prohibiting the appraiser from completing the appraisal, such as an inability to gain access to the property, you can address the matter and ensure that the appraisal is completed in time to complete the remaining tasks on the loan package.

   o   It is your job to assist the appraiser in the process whenever possible.

6. If for some reason the appraisal is not complete after 72 hours, call appraiser every 24 hours until appraisal is complete.

   o   If appraisal order is outstanding for more than one week, you need to begin searching for another appraiser partner.

This is an excellent example of the reason it is vital that your office develops a "relationship" with your affinity providers.

An appraisal that takes a week to complete can drastically slow your loan process.

Many lending professionals and real estate agents fail to remember the fact that the property is as important to the security of the loan being made as the borrower profile.

Ensuring that appraisals are remitted to underwriting promptly helps to speed the loan process, leads to better quality loan files, and enables your office to gain a reputation as the office that can get the job done smoothly, efficiently, and with fewer surprises.

Preliminary Title Reports

come from the Title Company who will insure the title of the home.

They research the property, seller, and borrower for any legal items, liens, or loans that may affect title to the property.

The completion of the preliminary title report typically takes between 1 and 2 weeks but you will wish to confirm the time requirements with the title company your office chooses to complete the abstract of title.

The title or settlement company may be chosen by

o   the real estate agent

o   the borrower

o   the seller

o   or your office

You may wish to ask the loan officer on the file if they have a title company preference.

A title company is an affinity service provider who sometimes refers potential borrowers to lending institutions.

The loan officer may have a specific title company with whom they are trying to build or strengthen a relationship.

In many areas, the title company and closing company are blended into one office.

Requesting title to a property from the company that will close the transaction requires the submittal of all of the transaction details, transaction documents, and loan program instructions.

The submittal of all of the necessary details and documents ensures that the company has all of the information that they need to complete the necessary title and closing functions within the timeline set on the sales agreement.

Title Request Form

DATE: _____ FROM: _____

TO: _____ FAX: _____

Borrower Name: _____

Phone Number: _____ SS#_____ SS#_____

Mailing Address: _____

Property Address: _____

Proposed Lender: _____ Loan Amount: _____

Purchase ___   Refinance ___   2nd Mortgage ___   Prepared by: _____

Current Owners: _____

Address: _____

Phone Number: _____ SS#_____ SS#_____

Estimated Close Date: _____
Purchase Price: $_____   Loan Amount: $_____
Attachments:

   1003
   Sales Agreement

   _____
   _____

6:7 Sample Form – Title Request Form

TITLE REQUEST PROCESS

In general, you will want to use a closing company with whom you have a comfortable working relationship. You will want to check with your branch manager to determine if the branch has established affinity relationships already in place that can benefit you when ordering Title Work.

When ordering title and closing services, you should use a form that incorporates all of the necessary information and details related to the title and closing functions. Your branch or closing company may have preferred forms available for your use. We have included a sample form that you may use to request closing and title services.

1.   You should fill out Title Request form completely.

Completing all entries will speed the process since the Title Company will not need to contact you for additional information.

2.   You should include all of the contact information and phone numbers for every individual concerned with the transaction. .You should include all of the contact details for

- o   Yourself
- o   The real estate agent
- o   The buyer
- o   The seller
- o   The closing department at the lenders offices
- o   Any inspection companies involved in the transaction
- o   Any other individual specific to the transaction

3.   When you send the title and closing request, you should also include the

- o   1003
- o   sales agreement
- o   any additional documentation specified by the closing company

You should confirm the documents that the company commonly requires before submitting any request.

4.   You should include any additional information such as the application of seller concessions that are specific to your transaction under the comments section of the request form.

Additional information included with the request should include any detail that is vital to the completion of the title work or closing.

You should always define any special loan characteristics that apply to your loan and define the closing costs concession and second mortgage information to ensure that the closing package is prepared correctly.

5.   You should log the date that you sent the request on the file tracking form.

Logging activity ensures proper documentation of all actions on a file and enables you to conduct follow-up activity if a delay or another issue arises at a later point in the transaction.

6.   Twenty-four hours after request has been sent you should receive a confirmation of the request from the company.

You should note this confirmation within the file tracking form and place the confirmation form in the file.

If you do not receive a confirmation, you should follow up with the closing company and note the follow up action and any information you receive from the company on the file tracking form.

7. One week to 10 days before closing, you should request the Title Commitment.

You may request the commitment verbally or with a fax request.

8. Upon receipt of the title commitment, you should contact the individual who will prepare the loan-closing package and confirm all of the transaction details. This confirmation helps to avoid calculations errors in the preparation of the closing documents. Some details to confirm include.

   o Sales Price
   o Loan Amount
   o Seller Concession
   o Estimated closing costs
   o Subordinate financing

9. Within 48 hours, the Title Commitment should be provided to you for submittal to underwriting.

When you receive the commitment, you should verify that there is a closing protection letter included.

10. You will place a copy of the wiring instructions for the closing company with the commitment.

If you use the same closing company for multiple transactions, they will typically provide you with a wiring instruction sheet that you can copy and attach to each file.

If you do not have a wiring instruction sheet for the closing company, contact the company offices to obtain one and then keep it for future use.

11. You will add the title commitment and wiring instructions to any remaining stipulations and submit the final file to underwriting for review.

12. Underwriting should clear any final conditions on the file at this time. If any stipulations remain outstanding, you will need to obtain the necessary documents to clear them.

You should log all contacts and conversations on the file tracking form so that any individual who accesses the file can immediately see the status of the processing activity relating to the transaction. This log also assist you in remember the actions that you have taken on a file and the date of the activity if an issue arises that creates a loan process delay.

Owners Policy Number: OP No: Reference No:

Lender's Policy No: LP No.

This Policy does not insure against loss or damage (and the Company will not pay costs, attorneys' fees or expenses) which arise by reason of the following:

Special Exceptions: The mortgage, if any, referred to in Item 4 of Schedule , and the following exceptions:

1.   Rights or claims of parties in possession not shown by the public records.

2.   Easements, or claims of easements, not shown by the public records.

3.   Any lien, or right to a lien, for services, labor, or materials heretofore or hereafter furnished, imposed by law and not shown by public records.

4.   Encroachments, overlaps, boundary line disputes, or other matters which would be disclosed by an accurate survey or inspection of the premises.

5.   Possible additional assessments for taxes for new construction or for any major improvements pursuant to provisions of Acts of Assembly relating thereto, not yet due and payable.

6.   Subject to all matters, notes, conditions, restrictions, easements, setback and building lines shown on map 0200-19-7B recorded in the Recorder of Deeds Office for THIS County.

7.   Subject to public and private rights in and to all roads and alleys, public or private, if any affecting the subject property.

THIS IS THE END OF SCHEDULE B

6:8 Sample Extraction – Title Insurance Schedule B

Homeowners Insurance

Your most important product is customer service. As an added service to customers, offices offer the service of obtaining Homeowner's Insurance quotes.

Many borrowers, especially the first time homebuyer, are uncertain of the process and information required to receive an Insurance quote and a binder. While this is not a typical part of your job, it is an added service that you can provide to the borrower that enhances their overall experience and satisfaction with your office.

Requesting an insurance quote for the borrower also enables you to build an additional affinity service relationship with the Insurance Agent.

Referring insurance quote requests to the Insurance Agent provides them with a possible source of business that they did not have previously. In providing this business source, you are setting the groundwork for a cross-referral program where they will refer borrowers to your office for their home lending needs.

It is important to remember to tell your borrower that you are performing this service on their behalf.

You MUST also tell the borrower that you are obtaining the quote for comparison purposes only and that they are under no obligation to use the service provider for their home insurance needs.

A sample of the Homeowner's Insurance requirements that might be set by underwriting is included to provide you with a better understanding of what homeowner's insurance stipulations may be required for the file.

A binder is required either before or at the closing.

Often the borrower will not have the time available to secure the entire homeowner's insurance policy. A binder showing proof that coverage has been obtained and a receipt showing proof the policy has been paid in full is sufficient to satisfy most underwriting requirements and enable the loan to proceed to closing.

Request for Homeowners Insurance Quote

Borrower : _____ Co-Borrower Name: _____

DOB: _____ DOB: _____

SSN: _____ SSN: _____

Mailing Address: _____

Home Phone: _____ Best Time to Call: _____

Property Address: _____

Value: _____ Sales Price: _____

Payment to be made: _____ Prior to Close _____ At Close

Expected Close Date: _____ Binder Needed By: _____

Proposed Lender: _____

Additional Comments: _____

Attachments:

_____1003
_____Credit Report
_____Sales Agreement
_____Appraisal

_____

_____

6:9 Sample Form – Homeowner's Insurance Quote Request

HAZARD INSURANCE REQUIREMENTS

Lender:

To: Escrow Officer

Date:
Escrow #:
Loan #:

Listed below are our Lenders policies, procedures and minimum requirements for Hazard Insurance, which must be provided covering the subject property. We will require that the insurance premium has been paid and date when renewal is due if property is a refinance.

1. Coverage required must be the lesser of the principal balance or the insurable value of the improvements. The coverage amount must fully compensate for any damage or loss on a replacement cost basis. If the loan program allows for potential negative amortization, the lender may require that the amount of coverage be increased to protect the amount of potential negative amortization.
2. The insurance company providing coverage must have an "A" rating or better in the latest edition of "Best's Insurance Guide", must be licensed in the State in which the property described above is located, and must be licensed to transact the lines of insurance required in the transaction.
3. Coverage shall provide at least Broad Form on one to four units, and at least "Vandalism and Malicious Mischief" over four units, with no deviation. Homeowner's policies must be equal to HO2 form.
4. Policies may contain deductibles on any peril as follows: Maximum deductible is the great of $1,000.00 or 1% of the coverage amount.
5. Policy must provide coverage for a term of at least one year. Premiums may be paid on an annual installment basis only if the policy provides the Lender will be notified in writing of cancellation 30 days prior to expiration of coverage, for any cause. Purchases: One year must be paid through escrow.
6. If an existing policy is provided and will expire within three months from recording, it must be renewed for the required term as noted above. These policies will be acceptable if they are current.
7. All forms and endorsements pertaining to the company requirements must appear on the Declaration page of the policy.
8. New policies must be accompanied by signed Broker of Record Authorization if borrower has recently changed insurance agents.
9. Verification of renewal of insurance policies must be in the Lenders office at least thirty days prior to the expiration date of the existing policy. If this requirement is not met, the LENDER OR ITS SUCCESSORS OR ASSIGNS MAY AT THEIR OPTION, BUT WITHOUT OBLIATION TO DO SO, PROVIDE COVERAGE TO REPLACE ANY EXPIRING POLIIES WHICH HAVE NOT BEEN PROPERLY RENEWED. The premium for such coverage will be remitted promptly by the undersigned, or Lender may charge borrower's account for the cost thereof.
10. Insurance agent's name, mailing address, and phone number must be on or attached to Binder/Policy.
11. Lender's Loss Payable Endorsement 438 BFU to be affixed in favor of:

12. Property address and insurance names to be designated as per ALTA Policy.
13. Our loan number must be shown on the policy and any subsequent endorsements.
14. Effective date of new policies, endorsements, and/or assignments shall be as of, or prior to, date of recording.
15. Please notify your agent to forward future premium notices directly to you.
16. If the security property is a condominium, larger than twenty units a fidelity bond in a minimum amount of at least equal to the sum of three months assessments on all units in the project for Directors and Officers is required. A copy of the master policy must be submitted to the Lender prior to funding.
17. The minimum amount of Flood Insurance required is the lesser of the outstanding principal balance of the loan, the full insurable value of the property, or the maximum amount of flood insurance available.

All policies, assignments, and or endorsements, for completion of our loan escrow are to be mailed to this lending office.

6:10 Sample Extraction – Lender's Insurance Requirements

KENNEY

Additional supporting documents	Additional paperwork may be needed on a case-by-case scenario.

The need for additional documents will vary by borrower's individual scenario and is one of the areas where you will await the stipulation list before requesting the documents.

As you gain in experience, you will become better able to anticipate what unusual documents underwriting may request, but for now, you will likely need to rely on the stipulation list. |
| Any Documents missing from initial loan application | You must also review the file package to ensure that you have requested and obtained any paperwork or documentation item that was missing from original loan application.

If the buyer or the seller is slow in providing the necessary documents, you may enlist the aid of the real estate agent in obtaining these items.

If an affinity service partner is slow in providing you with a necessary stipulation, you may need to discuss the services of the affinity service provider with your branch manager so that the speed of affinity services can be addressed and any issues resolved. |
| Escrow / Closing Instructions | Escrow or closing instructions are drawn up by the Escrow or settlement Company and they define the transaction and settlement details.

An Escrow or settlement company is an independent third party of the transaction that acts as the accountant. Some states call this the settlement company.

In California and some other states, a closing attorney or title company acts as the escrow or settlement agent.

The process of drawing up escrow instructions usually takes 2 to 7 days. |

Since all of these documents are secured from various companies and individuals, this is most often, where there are delays. This portion of the loan process will normally take 1 to 3 weeks.

Developing relationships with your various affinity providers is essential in speeding this process. It is also very important to have an effective pipeline management system and loan process follow up system in place. This allows you to easily order items from service providers. This will also enable you to follow up on missing items with Real Estate Agents and borrowers efficiently.

A typical Real Estate Transaction involves the timely cooperation of many different parties. Due to the number of people involved, there can be problems.

Since no loan is closed until it is closed, this list of items is potential roadblocks. It is very important for you to bear in mind that you are ultimately responsible for organizing the loan process and ensuring that it moves along in a timely manner.

Some of the delays are easily avoided with an adequate loan process follow up and reminder system and others will require you to build strong relationships with affinity service providers.

The Real Estate Agents could create delays in the loan process and closing if they

- do not get all documents signed promptly

- Did not structure the transaction properly

- Did not pre-qualify the borrower for motivation

- Misunderstand the borrowers needs or your instructions due to a lack of real estate experience

- Won't return phone calls

- Transfer to another office

- Goes on vacation leaving no one to handle the file

- Has poor people skills with the borrower

- Gets the borrower upset over minor points

- Does not communicate with their borrower, your office, the appraiser or the settlement company

The Escrow or Closing Company may cause delays if they

- Fail to notify the real estate agent or lender of unsigned or un-returned documents so that they can contact the individual responsible for the document and cure the problem

- Fails to obtain information from beneficiaries, lien holders, title companies, insurance companies, or lenders in a timely manner

- Incorrectly prepares paperwork

- Is incorrect at interpreting aspects of the transaction

- Passes incorrect assumptions about the transaction to other parties

- Lets the principals of the transaction leave town without getting all necessary signatures

- Is too busy or overscheduled

- Loses the paperwork related to the transaction

- Does not pass on valuable information fast enough

- Does not coordinate well so that many items can be done simultaneously

- Do not find liens or problems until last minute

The Inspection Company or The Appraiser can cause delays if they

- Are overly picky during the inspection

- Infuriates the seller

- Makes mistakes when preparing the documents or completing the inspection

- Delays completing their report

The Seller may create delays if they

- Lose motivation for the sale

- Nets less money from sale than they originally believed that they would

- Cannot find another home to purchase

- Has an unexpected occurrence such as an illness or divorce

- Fails to disclose or does not know about defects in the property

- Receive a Home inspection that reveals defects that the seller is unwilling to repair

- Removes property from the premises that the buyer believed was included in the sale

- Is unable to clear up problems or liens against the property

- Did not own 100% of property as disclosed

- Thought that the obtainment of partners signatures were "no problem" but they were

- Leaves town without giving power of attorney to another individual who can finalize the transaction on their behalf

- Uses a notary that did not make a clear stamp when notarizing their signatures

- Delays the projected move-out date

By building strong affinity service provider relationships, providing clear instructions to each party involved in the transaction, and carefully coordinating and following up on each aspect of the loan process, you can minimize many of these delays. It is vital that you maintain a constant awareness of the status of each loan package so that you can ensure that each party completes all of the steps necessary to move the package to a smooth closing meeting.

Once the Underwriting department has determined that all of the stipulations are acceptable and issued a satisfaction status, you will need to schedule the closing and request the closing documents.

The loan document process is the stage when the funding agent is preparing the loan documents. These loan documents are the legal binding documents to finalize the transaction.

They will include important items to be signed. Nearly every transaction will require the completion of the

Promissory Note	defining the amount borrowed, the interest rate charged, and the terms or repayment method applied to the loan, and the monthly payment amount.
Deed of Trust	that places the property as security to the loan and note
HUD 1	that provides an itemized breakdown of all fees incurred for obtaining the loan, all costs related to the transfer of the property and any other financial matter related to the sale.

The lender will typically also require that the borrower complete additional legal forms to help to confirm that the borrower understands the transaction, verify the borrower's statements during the loan process, and promote the security of the transaction.

Occupancy Declaration An occupancy declaration is a statement by the borrower that defines the use they intend to make of the property.

When a mortgage lender provides a mortgage loan, one aspect that will affect the approval is the use that the borrower intends to make of the property.

It is commonly believed that a borrower will make payments against their primary residence better than they will against a second home, investment property or other form of residence. As such, the entry that you make on the application form pertaining to occupancy plans of the property will change many aspects of the loan including interest rate, percentage of the value they will lend against and documentation requirements based on the occupancy plans of the borrower.

During the loan application process, the borrower will have provided information pertaining to the intended occupancy status of the property being transferred.

It is a common practice to request that the borrower complete a statement that confirming these occupancy plans during the settlement meeting.

This occupancy declaration will be included in nearly every closing package and it is essential that you have confirmed the occupancy plans of the borrower prior to remitting the initial application to the underwriting department for review.

A closing could be stopped if the borrower arrives and refuses to sign an occupancy declaration.

If you have conducted an adequate interview and completed the application forms properly, this document will have a limited impact on your closing.

OCCUPANCY DECLARATIONS

Lender:

RE: Loan No:
        PROPERTY ADDRESS:

The undersigned Borrower of the above described property does hereby declare, under penalty of perjury, as follows:

1.   Borrower shall occupy, establish, and use the Property as Borrowers principal residence within sixty days after execution of the Security Instrument and shall continue to occupy the property as Borrower's principal residence for at least one year after the date of occupancy unless Lender otherwise agrees in writing, which consent shall not be unreasonably withheld, or unless extenuating circumstances exist which are beyond the Borrower's control.

        You are hereby informed that Lender from time to time makes spot checks for owner occupancy on properties upon which we have secured a mortgage.

        Between the first and thirteenth day, after close of escrow, occupancy may be checked more than once. If after this check Lender is to believe that you never intended to occupy the subject as your primary residence, we may choose to call your note due and payable or increase your note rate by 100 basis points, in accordance with the applicable sections itemized on your note and Security Instrument and allowable by law.

2.   Borrower shall be in default, if during the loan application process, gave materially false or inaccurate information or statements to Lender (or failed to provide Lender with material information) in connection with the loan evidenced by the Note, including, but not limited to, representations concerning Borrower's occupancy of the Property as a Principal residence.

3.   The Lender has the right to foreclose on the loan under the terms of the Security Instrument if items 1 or 2 above are violated.

4.   Should Borrower's intention change prior to close of transaction, then it is agreed that the Lender will be immediately notified of that fact.

5.   Borrower understands that without this declaration of intention, Lender may not make the loan in connection with the property.

I DECLARE, UNDER PENALTY OF PERJURY, THAT THE FOREGOING DECLARATION IS TRUE AND CORRECT.

6:11 Sample Extraction – Occupancy Declaration – HUD Release

FEE DISCLOSURE	
APPLICANT(S) NAME AND ADDRESS	MORTGAGE BANKER/BROKER NAME AND ADDRESS
PROPERTY ADDRESS	TYPE OF LOAN

Today you have submitted a mortgage loan application to the Mortgage Banker or Broker listed above. All fees paid by you are nonrefundable. State law ( ) requires that the following information be disclosed to you.

The Mortgage Banker or Broker is required to refund all fees paid by an applicant borrower, other than those fees paid by the Mortgage Banker or Broker to a third party, when a mortgage loan is not produced within the time specified by the Mortgage Banker or Broker at the rate, term and overall cost agreed to by the borrower.

However, this provision shall not apply when the failure to produce a loan is due solely to the borrower's negligence, borrower's refusal to accept and close on a loan commitment or borrower's refusal or inability to provide information necessary for processing the loan, including, but not limited to, employment verifications and verifications of deposit.

This disclosure does not constitute approval of your loan or a commitment to make a loan to you.

6:11 Sample Extraction – Fee Disclosure – HUD Release

Fee Disclosure	Many lenders now require that the payment for certain fees be given to the lender by the buyer. These funds are held by the lender to pay for services that will be ordered in relationship to documenting the loan.
	Other fees may be paid directly to service providers during the transaction processing stage or paid out of the proceeds at the closing table.
Rate Lock	If the interest rate has already been locked-in; the document person draws the loan documents.
	If the interest rate has not been locked in, you should ensure that the form is completed at this time.

Document Prep	Once the loan documents are printed, they are then over-nighted to the Escrow Company or Settlement Company.
Schedule Meeting	The settlement agent then contacts the borrower with the final figures for the scheduled closing.
	This process from document order to signing will normally take 2-5 days.
Settlement	After the loan documents have been prepared, signed, dated, notarized, and returned, they will go into funding.
Funding	Funding is the time when all of the signed documents are reviewed by the lender to insure that everything is signed correctly.

At this point, they will also do a final back-up quality control check of your borrower's credit and employment to insure nothing has changed since the loan was approved.

Once everything has been verified and checked, the lender will fund the loan.

The funding of the loan is the time when the monies borrowed are wired to the closing company, escrow office, or the closing attorney for disbursement.

- o This is when the actual exchange of money is completed.

    This funding is usually completed through an electronic wire transfer.

- o Some lenders do dry closings in which the funds are not sent until all the review activity is complete.

In this case, the funding will usually take place 2 to 4 days after the loan documents have been returned to the lender by the closer.

- o In other cases, lenders send the funds to the escrow or closing company before the settlement meeting. If the funds are available at the settlement meeting, the escrow or closing agent will cut the checks and have them available for dispersal at the settlement table.

Recording	The recording process is the time that the legal, binding loan documents that were signed and notarized are taken to the county recorder office for recording.

The actual recording is simply, the time when the documents are time and date stamped by the county recorder office, recognized, and filed as an official public document.

The recording process usually takes place 24 to 48 hours after the loan has been funded and the electronic wire confirmed.

In some places a "special recording" or a same day recording may occur.

At this point, the loan is finalized and closed.

GLOSSARY OF MORTGAGE TERMS

1-year ARM: An adjustable-rate mortgage (ARM) that has an initial interest rate for one year, and thereafter has an adjustment interval of one year. The adjustment is based on comparison interest caps and the indexed rate

3/1 ARM: An adjustable-rate mortgage (ARM) that has an initial interest rate for three years, and thereafter has an adjustment interval of one year. The adjustment is based on comparison interest caps and the indexed rate.

5/1 ARM: An adjustable-rate mortgage (ARM) that has an initial interest rate for five years, and thereafter has an adjustment interval of one year. The adjustment is based on comparison interest caps and the indexed rate

7/1 ARM: An adjustable-rate mortgage (ARM) that has an initial interest rate for seven years, and thereafter has an adjustment interval of one year. The adjustment is based on comparison interest caps and the indexed rate

10/1 ARM: An adjustable-rate mortgage (ARM) that has an initial interest rate for ten years, and thereafter has an adjustment interval of one year. The adjustment is based on comparison interest caps and the indexed rate

Abstract of Title: A written history of all the transactions that bear on the title to a specific piece of land An abstract of title covers the time from when the property was first sold to the present. Used by the Title Company to produce a title binder

Acceleration Clause: The section of a mortgage document that allows the lender to speed up the payment date in the event of default, making the entire principal amount due

Acre: An area of land 43.560 square feet

Adjustable Rate Mortgage: Mortgage in which the rate of interest is adjusted based on a standard rate index. Most ARM's have caps on how much the interest rate may increase

Adjustment Interval: How often the loan's rate can be changed

Alternative Mortgage: 7/23 and 5/25 mortgages with a one-time rate adjustment after seven years and five years respectively Also known as a hybrid mortgage or a two-step mortgage

Amortization Schedule : A timetable for the gradual repayment of a mortgage loan An amortization schedule indicates the amount of each payment applied to interest and principal, and the remaining balance after each payment is made

Amortization Term: The amount of time required to amortize (repay) a mortgage loan. The amortization term is usually expressed in months. A 30-year fixed rate mortgage, for example, has an amortization term of 360 months

Annual Percentage Rate (APR): A standardized method of calculating the cost of a mortgage, stated as a yearly rate which includes such items as interest, mortgage insurance, and certain points or credit costs

Appraisal: A written report by a qualified appraiser estimating the value of the property

Appraised Value: An opinion of a property's fair market value, based on an appraiser's inspection and analysis of the property

Appraiser: A person qualified by education, training, and experience to estimate the value of real property

Appreciation: An increase in the value of a property due to changes in market conditions or improvements to the property

ARM: See Adjustable Rate Mortgage

Assessed Value: The value of a property as determined by a public tax assessor for the purpose of taxation

Assumable: A mortgage that a buyer can assume, or take over, from the seller of the property

Balloon Mortgage: A loan that has regular monthly payments, which amortize over a stated term but call for a final lump sum (balloon payment) at the end of a specified term, or maturity date such as 10 years

Basis Points: 1/100th of 1 percent If an interest rate changes 50 basis points, for example, it has move ½ of 1 percent

Binder: See title binder

Biweekly Mortgage: A mortgage that schedules payments every two weeks instead of the standard monthly payment The 26 biweekly payments are each equal to one-half of the monthly payment. The result for the borrower is a substantial reduction in interest payments because the mortgage is paid off sooner. See also prepayment plan

Bridge loan: A loan that "bridges" the gap between the purchase of a new home and the sale of the borrower's current home. The borrower's current home is used as collateral and the money is used to close on the new home before the current home is sold. Some are structured so they completely pay off the old home's first mortgage at the bridge loan's closing. Others pile the new debt on top of the old. They usually run for a term of six months

Broker: See mortgage broker

Broker Premium: A premium paid to the mortgage broker as the "middleman" in the mortgage process between the lender and the borrower

Built-ins: Cabinets, ranges, ceiling fans and other items permanently attached to the structure, and which a buyer may assume will remain with the structure

Buy down: The process of trading money for a lower mortgage rate The borrower "buys down" the interest rate on a mortgage by paying discount points up front. It can also be a mortgage in which an initial lump sum payment is made to reduce a borrower's monthly payments during the first few years of a mortgage

Caps: The maximum amount the interest rate can change annually or cumulatively over the life of an adjustable rate mortgage. F or example, if the caps are 2 percent annual and 6 percent life of loan, a mortgage with a first-year rate of 10 percent could rise to no more than 12 percent the second year, and no more than 16 percent over the entire life of the loan

Certificate of Title: A statement provided by the Title Company or attorney stating that the title to the real estate is legally held by the current owner

Chattel: Personal property

Clear title: A title that is free of liens or legal questions as to ownership of a piece of property

Closing: The meeting at which the sale of a property is finalized The buyer signs the lender agreement for the mortgage and pays' closing costs and escrow amounts. The buyer and seller sign documents to transfer the ownership of the property. Also known as the settlement

Closing costs: Expenses incurred by buyers and sellers in transferring ownership of a property. Closing costs normally include an origination fee, an attorney's fee, taxes, escrow payments, and charges for title insurance. Lenders or Real Estate Agents provide estimates of closing costs to prospective homebuyers

Closing Statement: A financial disclosure accounting for all funds changing hands at the closing See also HUD-1 Statement

Cloud on title: Any fact or condition that could adversely affect the title

Commission: In real estate, the broker, or mortgage associates fee for assisting in the transaction Usually expressed as a percentage of the total paid by the buyer

Commitment: A formal offer by a lender stating the approved terms for lending money to a homebuyer

Common Area Assessment: A levy against individual unit owners in a condominium or planned unit development to pay for upkeep, repairs, and improvements to the property's common areas, such as corridors, elevators, parking lots, swimming pools and tennis courts

Comparables: Refers to "comparable properties" which are used for comparative purposes in the appraisal process. Comps are recently sold properties that are similar in size, location, and amenities to the home for sale. Comps help an appraiser determine the fair market value of a property

Condominium: A real estate project in which each unit owner has title to a unit of the project, and sometimes and undivided interest in the common areas

Conforming Loan: A loan that conforms to the standard rules for purchase by Freddie Mac or Fannie Mae

Contingency: A condition that must be met before a contract is legally binding. For example, homebuyers often include a contingency that specifies that the contract is not binding until after a satisfactory report from a home inspector

Contract: In real estate parlance, the contract is the legal document by which buyer and seller make offers and counteroffers. The real estate contract describes the property, includes or excludes items in the property, names the price, apportions the closing costs between the parties and sets forth a closing date. When a buyer and seller agree on the terms and sign the same document the property is said to be "under contract". More formally known as the agreement for the sale, purchase agreement, or earnest money contract

Conventional Mortgage: Usually refers to a fixed-rate, 30-year mortgage that is not insured by FHA, Farmers Home Administration, or Veterans Administration

Convertible Mortgage: An adjustable rate mortgage ARM that can be converted to a fixed mortgage under specific conditions

Cooperative: A type of multiple ownership in which the residents of a multiunit housing complex own shares in the cooperative corporation that owns the property, giving each resident the right to occupy a specific apartment or unit

Cost-of-funds: A yield index based upon the cost of funds to savings & loan institution in the San Francisco Federal Home Loan Bank District. It is one of the indexes commonly used to set the rate of adjustable rate mortgages

Covenant: A written restriction on the use of land, most commonly in use today in homeowners associations

Credit report: A report on a person's credit history prepared by a credit bureau and used by a lender in determining a loan applicant's record for paying debts in a timely manner

Debt-to-Income Ratio: The percentage of a person's monthly earnings used to pay off all debt obligations Lenders consider two ratios, constructed in slightly different ways. The first called the front-end ratio, the ratio of the monthly housing expenses – including principal, interest, property taxes, and insurance, (PITI) is compared to the borrower's gross, pretax monthly income. In the back-end ratio, a borrower's other debts such as auto loans and credit cards are figured in. Lenders usually consider both and set an acceptable ratio. Some lenders and some lending qualifying agencies only consider the back-end ratio

Deed: The legal document conveying title to the property

Depreciation: A decline in the value of a property as opposed to appreciation

Discount Points: A type of point (1 percent of the loan) paid by the borrower to reduce the interest rate

Down payment: The amount of a property's purchase price that the buyer pays in cash and does not finance with a mortgage

Earnest money: A deposit made by potential homebuyers during negotiations with the seller. The sum shows a seller that the buyer is serious about purchasing a property

Easement: The right of another to use a property The most common easements are for utility lines

80-10-10 Loan: A combination of an 80 percent loan-to-value first mortgage, a 10 percent down payment and a 10 percent home equity loan. This is also sometimes referred to as a CLTV (Combined Loan-to-Value)

Encumbrance: A lien, charge, or liability against a property

Equal Credit: A federal law that requires lenders and other creditors to make credit equally available with out discrimination based on race, color, religion, national origin, age, sex, marital status, or receipt of income from public assistance programs

Equity: The value of a homeowner's unencumbered interest in real estate Equity is the difference between the homes fair market value and the unpaid balance of the mortgage and any outstanding liens Equity increases as the mortgage is paid down or as the property enjoys appreciation

Escrow Payment: The portion of a homeowner's monthly mortgage payment that is held by the loan servicer to pay for taxes and insurance Also known as reserves The loan servicer holds the escrow funds separately from money meant to pay principal and interest

Fair Credit Reporting Act: A consumer protection law that regulates the disclosure of consumer credit reports by credit reporting agencies and establishes procedures for correcting mistakes on a person's credit record

Fannie Mae: Nickname for Federal National Mortgage Association It is a government-chartered non-bank financial services company and the nation's largest source of financing for home mortgages It was started to make sure mortgage money is available in all areas of the country

FHA Mortgage: A mortgage insured by the Federal Housing Administration

First mortgage: A mortgage that is the primary lien against a property

Fixed-rate Mortgage: A mortgage in which the interest rate does not change during the entire term of the loan, most often 15, or 30 years

Flood Insurance   Insurance that compensates for the physical property damage resulting from rising water It is required for properties located in federally designated flood areas

Foreclosure: The legal process by which a homeowner in default on a mortgage is deprived of interest in the property This usually involves a forced sale of the property at public auction with the proceeds of the sale being applied to the mortgage debt

Freddie Mac: Nickname for Federal Home Loan Mortgage Corp A financial corporation chartered by the federal government to buy pools of mortgages from lenders and sell securities backed by these mortgages

Ginnie Mae: Nickname for the Government National Mortgage Association

Good Faith Estimate: A written estimate of closing costs that the lender must provide to prospective homebuyers within three days of submitting a mortgage loan application

Government National Mortgage Association (Ginnie Mae) A government-owned corporation within the US Department of Housing and Urban Development (HUD) Created by Congress in 1968, GNMA has responsibility for the special assistance loan program known as Ginnie Mae

Hazard Insurance: Insurance coverage that compensates for physical damage to property from natural disasters such as fire and other hazards Depending on where a piece of property is located, lenders may also require flood insurance or policies covering windstorms (hurricanes) or earthquakes

Home Inspection: An inspection by a building professional that evaluates the structural and mechanical condition of a property

Homeowners Association: A nonprofit association that manages the common areas of a condominium or PUD Unit owners pay the association a fee to maintain areas owned jointly

Homeowner's Insurance: An insurance policy that combines personal liability insurance and hazard insurance coverage for a residence and its contents

Housing Expense: The percentage of gross monthly income that goes toward paying a Ratio mortgage or rent on a home

HUD-1: The document with an itemized listing of closing costs payable at the closing or settlement meeting when buying property The closing costs can include a commission, loan fees, and points, and sums set aside for escrow payments, taxes, and insurance It is signed by both the buyer and the seller, who may be paying some of the closing costs The statement form is published by HUD

Hybrid Mortgage: See alternative mortgage products.

Index: A published measure of the cost of money that lenders use to calculate the rate on an ARM The most common indexes are the one-year Treasury Constant Maturity Yield and the FHLB 11th District Cost of Funds

Indexed Rate: The sum of the published index plus the margin For example, if the index were 9 percent and the margin 2.75 percent, the indexed rate would be 11.75 percent. Often, lenders charge less than the indexed rate the first year of an ARM

Initial Interest Rate: Starting rate of an ARM

Interest Tax Deduction: Most mortgage holders can deduct all the interest paid on the loan in filing income tax The deduction applies to people with just on mortgage on a primary residence, as well as those with a combination of loans. Within certain time limits set by the IRS, points paid up front on a mortgage are usually deductible in the year the house was purchased

Jumbo Mortgage: Mortgages larger than the limits set by Fannie Mae and Freddie Mac. A jumbo mortgage will carry a higher interest rate than a conventional mortgage

Lease-purchase   A financing option that allows a potential homebuyer to lease a property with the option to buy   Often constructed so the monthly rent payment covers the owner's first mortgage payment, plus an additional amount as a savings deposit to accumulate cash for a down payment   A seller may agree to a lease-purchase option if the housing market is saturated and the seller is having a difficult time selling the property

Lien: A legal hold or claim from one person on the property of another   The lien placed by a first mortgage is special. It is called a first lien and takes precedence over others

Lifetime Rate Cap: In an ARM, it limits the amount that the interest rate can increase or decrease over the life of the loan. See also caps

Lis Pendens: A pending lawsuit; in real estate, the constructive notice filed in public records that a legal dispute exists over a piece of property

Livery of Seizen: Under common law, the process of transferring title

Loan Origination: The process by which a mortgage lender obtains a mortgage secured by real property An origination fee is charged by the lender to process all forms involved in obtaining a mortgage

Loan-to-value (LTV) Ratio: The ratio of a mortgage loan amount to the property's appraised value or selling price, whichever is less For example, if a home is sold for $100,000 and the mortgage amount is $80,000 the LTV is 80%

Lock: Lender's guarantee that the mortgage rate quoted will be good for a specific amount of time. The homebuyer usually wants the lock to stay in effect until the date of the closing

Lock-and-Float: Rate programs offered by companies that allow borrowers to lock in the current interest rate on a mortgage for a specified period, while also letting them "float" the rate down if market conditions improve before closing

Low-down Mortgages: Mortgages with a low down payment, usually less than 10 percent. Frannie Mae and Freddie Mac design loan programs that spell out a set of standards for lenders. In recent years, these government-chartered agencies have made low-down mortgages more available

Margin: The number of percentage points added to the index on a one-year ARM

Maturity : The date on which the principal balance of a loan becomes due and payable

Mortgage: A legal document that uses property as collateral to secure payment of a debt

Mortgage Banker: The lender that originates a mortgage loan, the one making the loan directly, and closing the loan

Mortgage Broker: An individual or company that brings borrowers and lenders together for the purpose of loan origination Unlike a mortgage banker, brokers do not fund the loan but work on behalf of several lenders. Brokers typically require a fee or a commission for their service See broker premium

Mortgage Insurance: A policy that insures the lender against loss should the homeowner default on a mortgage. Depending on the loan, the insurance can be issued by government agencies such as the FHA or a private company. It is part of the monthly mortgage payment. (See also private mortgage insurance PMI)

Negative Amortization: A gradual increase in mortgage debt that happens when a monthly payment does not cover the entire principal and interest due The shortfall is added to the remaining balance to create "negative" amortization

No-doc or low-doc Loan: These no-documentation or low-documentation loans are designed for the entrepreneur or self-employed, for recent immigrants with money in foreign countries or for borrowers who cannot or choose not to reveal information about their incomes

Note: The document giving evidence of mortgage indebtedness, including the amount and terms of repayment

Origination Fee: A fee paid to the lender for processing a loan application

Owner financing A transaction in which the seller of a house provides all or part of the financing Sellers may provide financing because they need to sell the property right away or they are having difficulty selling the house and want to provide financing as an incentive to a buyer

Periodic rate cap: In an ARM, it limits how much an interest rate can increase or decrease during any one-adjustment period See also caps

PITI: Stands for principal, interest, taxes and insurance that are the usual components of a monthly mortgage payment

PITI Reserves: A cash amount that a homebuyer must have on hand after making a down payment and paying all closing costs. The reserves required by a lender must equal the amount a buyer would pay for PITI for a specific number of months

Plat: A map that shows a parcel of land and how it is subdivided into individual lots Plat maps also show the locations of streets and easements

PMI: See private mortgage insurance

Points: A point equals 1 percent of a mortgage loan. Lenders charge points as a way to make a profit. Borrowers may pay discount points to reduce the loan interest rate. Buyers are prohibited from paying points on HUD or VA guaranteed loans

Pre-approval: This process goes a step further than pre-qualification. It means the lender has contacted the borrower's employer, bank, and other places to verify all claims of earnings and assets. In return, the borrower receives a letter stating the lender is willing to grant a mortgage for a specific amount within a limited period with the stipulation that there are no material changes to the borrower's situation

Prepayment Penalty: A fee imposed by certain lenders if the first mortgage is paid off early

Prepayment Plan: Similar to biweekly mortgage, but operated by a third party In it, the borrower pays to the third party, half the monthly mortgage payment every two weeks At the end of the year, the plan operators typically take the extra money that results from the process and sends lump sum payment to the participants' lenders

Pre-qualification: An early evaluation by a lender of a potential homebuyer's credit report, plus earnings, savings, and debt information The homebuyer gets a non-binding estimate of the mortgage amount the borrower would qualify for, or how much house the borrower can afford. Buyers who pre-qualify can go a step further and seek a pre-approval

Rate Lock: A commitment issued by a lender to the homebuyer or the mortgage broker guaranteeing a specific interest rate for a specified amount of time See also lock

Real Estate Agent: A person licensed to negotiate and transact the sale of real estate on behalf of the property owner

RESPA: Real Estate Settlement Procedures Act A consumer protection law that requires lenders to give homebuyers advance notice of closing costs, which are payable at the closing or settlement meeting

Realtor: A real estate broker or an associate who holds an active membership in a local real estate board that is affiliated with the National Association of Realtors

Refinancing: Securing a new loan in order to pay off the existing mortgage or to gain access to the existing equity in the home

Roll-in Loan: A refinance loan that rolls any closing costs or fees into the loan. These programs best serve people who have a reasonable amount of equity, want to reduce their overall interest expense, and plan to stay in their homes

Rural Housing Service (RHS): The agency in the US Department of Agriculture providing financing to farmers and other qualified borrowers buying property in rural areas who are unable to obtain loans elsewhere. It offers low-interest-rate loans with no down payment to borrowers with low-to-moderate incomes who live in rural areas or small towns

Sales Agreement: A written contract signed by the buyer and the seller of a house stating the terms and conditions under which the property will be sold

Second Mortgage: A mortgage on the property that has a lien position behind the first mortgage

Servicer: An organization that collects monthly mortgage principal and interest payments from homeowners and manages escrow accounts for paying taxes and homeowners' insurance premiums The servicer often services mortgages that have been purchased by an investor in the secondary mortgage market

Settlement: See closing

Sub-prime Mortgage: A mortgage granted to a borrower considered sub-prime, that is, a person with a less-than perfect credit report. Sub-prime borrowers either have missed payments on a debt or have been late with payments. Lenders charge a higher interest rate to compensate for potential losses from customers who may run into trouble and default

Time is of the Essence: A phrase inserted in contracts to require a punctual performance

Title: A legal document proving a person's right to claim entitlement to a property, including the history of the property's ownership

Title Binder: Written evidence of temporary title insurance coverage

Title Company: A company that specializes in examining and insuring titles to real estate

Title insurance: Insurance that protects against loss from disputes over ownership of a property. A policy may protect the mortgage lender and/or the homebuyer

Title search: A check of title records to ensure that the seller is the legal owner of a property and that there are no liens or other claims against the property

Transfer Tax: State or local tax levied when title passes from one owner to another

Treasury Index: An index used to determine interest rate changes for certain ARM mortgages. It is based on the results of auctions that the US Treasury holds for its Treasury bills and securities or is derived from the US Treasury's daily yield curve, which is based on the closing market bid yields on actively traded Treasury securities in the over-the-counter market

Truth-in-Lending Act (TILA): A federal law that requires lenders to disclose, in writing, the terms and conditions of a mortgage, including the annual percentage rate APR and other charges

Underwriter: A company or person undertaking the responsibility for issuing a mortgage Underwriters analyze a borrower's credit worthiness and set the loan amount

VA Mortgage: A loan backed by the Veterans Administration. It requires very low or no down payments and has less stringent requirements for qualification. Members of the US armed forces are eligible for the loans under certain qualifying conditions

Wraparound Mortgage: A new mortgage that includes the remaining balance on the old mortgage plus a new amount

KENNEY

MORTGAGE LENDING APPENDIX C

Loan Processor Study Workbook

Chapter 1 - The Lending Process

1.   What are the two classifications within the mortgage market/

_____

_____

_____

2.   What is an investing pool?

_____

_____

_____

3.   What are the three most common employment opportunities for a loan processor?

_____

_____

_____

_____

4.   What is the purpose of a mortgage brokerage?

_____

_____

_____

_____

5.   What are the most common entities within the secondary mortgage market/

_____

_____

_____

_____

6.   Which is not a common entity within the primary mortgage market?
   a.   Mortgage Brokerage Office
   b.   Mutual Savings Bank
   c.   Credit Union
   d.   Insurance Company

Chapter 2 – Ethics and Disclosure

1. What is the purpose of the laws that govern the ethics and disclosures with which you handle loan processes?

2. What is HMDA?

3. What is the purpose of fair housing laws?

4. What other act assists in the prevention of discrimination against applicants?

5. What items are illegal for use in evaluating applicant's qualifications?

6. What are the three common notices you might provide an applicant with regard to their credit application?

Mortgage Lending – Home Mortgage Loan Processing

7. What is RESPA?

_____

_____

_____

_____

8. What is the disclosure notice requirement if a loan is transferred to a new servicer?

_____

_____

_____

_____

9. What is a settlement statement?

_____

_____

_____

_____

10. What is TILA?

_____

_____

_____

_____

11. When must a right to cancel be provided?

_____

_____

_____

_____

12. Explain the reason for HOEPA.

_____

_____

_____

_____

13.   When will PMI be automatically cancelled in a normal risk mortgage?

_____

_____

_____

_____

14.   When will PMI be automatically cancelled in a high-risk mortgage?

_____

_____

_____

_____

15.   Why have ethics and disclosure laws been created?

    a.   To provide the lender with a series of practical directions
    b.   To protect the interest of the public
    c.   To make the obtainment of mortgage funds a fair practice
    d.   All of the above

16.   The Loan Processor must:

    a.   educate the consumer
    b.   act in an ethical manner
    c.   incorporate the required practices into their daily workload
    d.   all of the above

17.   Many states have created educational and licensure requirements for lending professionals.

    a.   True
    b.   False

18.   HMDA requires the reporting of

    a.   pipeline reports
    b.   loan origination referral data
    c.   public loan data
    d.   none of the above

19.   Information for the HMDA reports should be gathered:

    a.   at the closing table
    b.   at the time of pre-qualification
    c.   at the initial application
    d.   during post-close processes

20. Fair housing laws are designed to prevent

 a. discrimination in a credit related transaction
 b. discrimination in the setting of application appointments
 c. too many underprivileged loan disbursements
 d. none of the above

21. ECOA is

 a. equal credit origination act
 b. every credit opportunity agenda
 c. equal credit opportunity act
 d. none of the above

22. ECOA addresses:

 a. discriminatory actions
 b. predatory lending tactics
 c. required action disclosures
 d. all of the above

23. RESPA

 a. Helps consumers shop for settlement services
 b. Eliminates referral fees
 c. Requires specific borrower disclosures
 d. All of the above

24. A point is .10 percent of the loan amount

 a. True
 b. False

25. The borrower has the right to cancel any credit transaction involving their home within 3 days of the funding of the transaction.

 a. True
 b. False

26. All borrowers must purchase flood insurance

 a. True
 b. False

Chapter 3 - Prequalification

1. What is the primary reason that many loan Processors fail to obtain the information that will be needed for a pre-qualification?

_____

_____

_____

_____

2. What is the essential element to gaining the information you need from a borrower?

_____

_____

_____

3. Why is the initial contact with any potential borrower important?

_____

_____

_____

_____

4. Why should you request referral information of each pre-qualification?

_____

_____

_____

_____

5. Why do you ask if the applicant has chosen a home to purchase during the pre-qualification interview?

_____

_____

_____

_____

6. What is your most important product?

_____

_____

_____

_____

7. Most loan inquiries are taken
   a. by the underwriter
   b. by the loan Processor
   c. over the telephone
   d. both b & c

8. Your most valuable tool in planning a loan strategy is
   a. customer service skills
   b. information
   c. qualification skills
   d. loan knowledge

9. The pre-approval questionnaire contains
   a. all of the information you will need from the borrower
   b. most of the information you will need for the loan application
   c. all of the information the underwriting team will require
   d. most of the information necessary to close the loan

10. The initial contact
    a. sets the tone for your relationship with the borrower
    b. is the most essential information-gathering period
    c. sets the loan program you will use for the borrower
    d. none of the above

11. You will request a credit authorization verbally before pulling borrower credit.
    a. True
    b. False

12. You may enter common nicknames for the borrower
    a. True
    b. False

13. You must always have a co-borrower for the loan
    a. True
    b. False

14. You should complete the pre-qualification questionnaire as soon as the borrower locates the home they wish to purchase
    a. True
    b. False

15. The most important lending product is
    a. low rate loans and fixed products
    b. professionalism and responsiveness
    c. varied products with low down payment
    d. none of the above

16. The pre-qualification questionnaire will provide you with
    a. answers to every question on the questionnaire
    b. information that will be noted in the explanation of credit section
    c. all of the required documentation
    d. none of the above

Chapter 5 – Loan Process

1.   What are the three common written decisions you will see from underwriting?

_____

_____

_____

_____

_____

2.   What is an affinity provider?

_____

_____

_____

_____

3.   Who is ultimately responsible for the smooth process and timely closing of the loan?

_____

_____

_____

_____

_____

4.   How can you avoid loan process delays?

_____

_____

_____

_____

5.   How can you foster positive relationships with affinity service providers?

_____

_____

_____

_____

6.   The underwriter will review all aspects of the file including:
   a.   Source of down payment
   b.   The borrower's personal recommendations
   c.   The borrower's professional references
   d.   All of the above

7. The underwriter will review the file and issue an
   a.   approval
   b.   denial
   c.   conditional approval
   d.   Any of the above

8. Prior to closing documents must be provided to the underwriter before the loan documents can be requested.

   a.   True
   b.   False

9. The processing stage is a stage where
   a.   all information is verified and submitted
   b.   missing documentation is requested
   c.   data is transferred to the underwriter
   d.   all of the above

10. A verification of deposit is a form sent
   a.   To the closing or settlement agent to verify the funds to close
   b.   To the bank to verify the average bank account balance of the borrower
   c.   to the real estate agent to verify the earnest money deposit
   d.   none of the above

11. The funding is when
   a.   the underwriter completes a final loan review
   b.   the monies borrowed are wired or sent to the closing agent
   c.   the monies borrowed are disbursed to the proper individuals
   d.   none of the above

12. Delays in the loan process can be avoided by
   a.   implementing a loan process follow-up and reminder system
   b.   creating strong relationships with affinity service providers
   c.   efficient pipeline management
   d.   all of the above

13. Many loan Processors forget to create
   a.   a good closing team
   b.   an adequate filing system
   c.   positive service relationships
   d.   borrower commitment

14. An affinity service provider includes any individual who must accomplish tasks in a timely and professional manner in order for you to accomplish your goal of closed loans.
   a.   True
   b.   False

15. You should treat your affinity service providers
   a.   Respectfully
   b.   Friendly
   c.   With Consideration
   d.   All of the above

Chapter 5 – Documentation

1.   What is HUD and what is their function?

_____

_____

_____

_____

2.   What is PMI?

_____

_____

_____

3.   What is the annual mortgage-insurance premium?

_____

_____

_____

_____

4.   Gross income is:

_____

_____

_____

_____

5.   What is a compensating factor and why is it important?

_____

_____

_____

6.   Why must you request income documentation from each borrower?

_____

_____

_____

7.   What does the mortgage or rental history tell the loan underwriter?

_____

_____

_____

_____

8.   What is a VOM?

_____

_____

_____

_____

9.   What is a CLTV?

_____

_____

_____

_____

10.   Explain the general rule regarding credit risk and borrower investment.

_____

_____

_____

_____

11.   Why should you request all borrower documentation at the beginning of the loan process?

_____

_____

_____

_____

12.   Why is it important to document each loan package you submit?

_____

_____

_____

_____

13. Why should you note any missing information on the loan cover letter that you submit with the package?

_____

_____

_____

_____

14. Why should you include compensating factor information at the time of the initial submittal even when an exception request is not expected?

_____

_____

_____

_____

15. Why should you include information regarding the approval and transaction specifics you are requesting as part of your loan cover sheet?

_____

_____

_____

_____

16. What is the purpose of a stipulation list?

_____

_____

_____

_____

17. In 1937, what agency was created to provide more families with the opportunity to become homeowners?
   a. Federal Housing Acceptance
   b. Federal Homeowners Association
   c. Federal Housing Administration
   d. Federal Housing Authority

18. The down payment for a purchase under most conventional guidelines may be obtained as a gift from
   a. A small local lender
   b. A family member
   c. A for profit agency designed to assist in securing down payment funds
   d. The government

19. Under most conventional, a borrower's monthly payments toward the home should not exceed what percentage of the gross monthly income?
    a.   25%
    b.   31%
    c.   29%
    d.   27%

20. HUD is a direct lender
    a.   True
    b.   False

21. The automatic insurance premium cancellation requires that the principal balance of the loan fall below:
    a.   78%
    b.   85%
    c.   80%
    d.   75%

22. Overtime and bonus income may be used to qualify a borrower providing there is:
    a.   A one-year history
    b.   A three-year history
    c.   A two-year history
    d.   A verbal history

23. What type of rental income is an acceptable source of income?
    a.   Income from roommates
    b.   Income from boarders
    c.   Rent received by parents
    d.   Income from an investment property received under a lease

24. What percentage of business must a borrower own to be considered self-employed?
    a.   25%
    b.   75%
    c.   90%
    d.   85%

25. A borrower may choose to use alimony, child support, or separate maintenance if they provide what documentation?
    a.   12 month payment history from the courts
    b.   Evidence that the payments will continue for at least three years
    c.   Court documents showing who was awarded the largest portion of the overall assets
    d.   Both A & B

26. Mortgage or rental history is often used to project the probability of a borrower repaying their new mortgage in a timely manner.
    a.   True
    b.   False

27. If the mortgage or rental history is not included in the credit report, which of the following is an acceptable replacement?
   a. Verification forms sent to the mortgage holder or rental management company, if these are an entity not an individual to verify the history of the account
   b. A letter from the landlord or mortgage holder saying the rent or mortgage payment was received in a timely manner
   c. 12 months cancelled rent checks showing a timely payment to an individual landlord or mortgage holder
   d. Both A & C

28. Bank statement as income documentation programs are typically not penalized with a higher interest or down payment requirement because the statements are considered full documentation.
   a. True
   b. False

29. An outright gift of money toward a purchase of a home is typically acceptable if it is a gift from:
   a. A charitable organization
   b. A small loan
   c. A credit card
   d. None of the above

30. The loan Processor is the liaison between
   a. the borrower and the loan funder
   b. the borrower and underwriting
   c. the broker and underwriting
   d. the lender and the broker

31. Each time you submit a stipulation the underwriter will
   a. review the entire loan file
   b. request additional documentation
   c. complain about the documentation
   d. request a different stipulation

32. If you must repeatedly return to the borrower for additional documentation you will gain
   a. borrower loyalty
   b. a poor reputation
   c. underwriting approval
   d. all of the above

33. The underwriting summary is a form of
   a. checklist of inclusions
   b. guideline
   c. application overview
   d. none of the above

34. When requesting an appraisal you should note
   a. the borrowers approval rating
   b. the method of billing and payment
   c. the title company who will close the loan
   d. the possibility of a field review

35. The most important product a Loan Processor has available is
    a. low interest rates
    b. fast underwriting approvals
    c. customer service skills
    d. the ability to relate well to borrowers

36. The first act you will take on a loan package is to
    a. pull the credit report
    b. review the application
    c. complete the pre-qualification
    d. send VOE/VOR/VOM forms

37. You should revise the good faith estimate
    a. frequently throughout the loan process
    b. upon altering any borrower credit specifics
    c. upon receipt of the sales agreement
    d. upon receipt of the initial loan approval

38. The borrower should be informed of the final loan specifics
    a. before the closing
    b. the day of closing
    c. at the closing table
    d. none of the above

39. The loan processor should take gifts to the closing
    a. True
    b. False

40. What is automatic underwriting? _____
    _____
    _____
    _____
    _____

41. What does automatic underwriting consider? _____
    _____
    _____
    _____

42. What is the largest benefit of automatic underwriting from the perspective of the loan processor? ____
    _____
    _____
    _____

43. How is this benefit accomplished?

_____

_____

_____

_____

44. What is your primary function in relationship to automatic underwriting?

_____

_____

_____

45. What occurs if a loan submittal is not approved through automatic underwriting?

_____

_____

_____

46. Automatic underwriting negates the need for a loan processor to review the file.
    a. True
    b. False

47. Automatic underwriting makes its determination by reviewing
    a. Debt ratios
    b. Credit history
    c. Collateral
    d. All of the above

48. Automatic underwriting relies on
    a. Loan Processor opinion and documentation
    b. underwriting guideline matrix compared to borrower criteria
    c. historical loan performance and statistical models
    d. all of the above

49. Underwriting proceeds less smoothly through the use of automatic underwriting
    a. True
    b. False

50. Two primary focuses of automatic underwriting are:
    a. Profit and loss
    b. Speed and fairness
    c. Interest and Fees
    d. Origination closings

51.   When a loan does not meet the requirements of automatic underwriting, it will be
    a.   Denied
    b.   Conditionally approved
    c.   Submitted traditionally
    d.   Altered to conform to the requirements

MORTGAGE LENDING APPENDIX D

Loan Processor Workbook Answer Keys

Chapter 1 - The Lending Process

1. Primary Mortgage MarketSecondary Mortgage Market
2. A group of smaller investors seeking a low risk, long term investment and having capital available to purchase packaged loan products
3. Bank   Brokerage Office   E Commute
4. To act as a liaison between the borrowers seeking mortgage funds and multiple funding sources.
5. Insurance Companies   Pension funds   Individual investors
   Primary Lenders with excess deposits
6. d.

Chapter 2 – Ethics and Disclosure

1. To protect the interest of the public and make the obtainment of housing and home mortgage funds a fair practice for all applicants.
2. The home mortgage disclosure act
3. To prevent discrimination against any borrower in the sale, rental, financing, or other housing related transaction
4. The equal credit opportunity act
5. Race, color, religion, sex, national origin, marital status, age, source of income, handicap, and familial status
6. Approval, counter-offer, or denial
7. Real Estate Settlement Procedures Act, which helps consumers shop for settlement services and eliminates referral fees that increase the costs of certain settlement services
8. 15 days
9. The HUD 1 is a statement that itemizes all closing costs payable at the closing or settlement meeting.
10. The truth-in-lending act that is part of the consumer credit protection act. The act is meant to protect and inform the consumer by requiring specific disclosures regarding the loan terms and costs.
11. Any credit transaction that involves a security interest in a borrower's primary residence must provide the borrower with the right to rescind.
12. The homeowner's equity protection act is designed to protect a borrower against unfair and abusive lending tactics.
13. When the borrower's equity position reaches 22% if the borrower is current on mortgage payments or when the borrower reaches a 22% or greater equity position and the borrower brings their mortgage obligations current.
14. When the loan reaches a 77%, LTV or the loan reaches the half-life whichever occurs first in time.

15.	D	16.	D	17.	A	18.	C	19.	C	20.	A
21.	C	22.	D	23.	D	24.	B	25.	B	26.	B

Chapter 3 – Prequalification

1. Because they are afraid to ask for information

2. You must ask for the information
3. The initial contact sets the tone for the entire relationship with that borrower. Most people will make decisions concerning your professionalism and character within the first 30 seconds of contact.
4. To assist in tracking referral source information, assessing marketing and advertising effectiveness and to provide follow-up information regarding the applicant to the referral source
5. This question enables you to assess the urgency of the query and determine if the borrower thus enabling you to prioritize the flow of work within your office.
   You will also be able to determine if the borrower is working with an agent thereby strengthening referral relationships.
   If the borrower has chosen a home, you will be able to use real purchase numbers to assess DTI and borrower expectations prior to the first face-to-face meeting.
6. The professionalism, attentiveness, and responsiveness you provide to your borrowers.

7.	D	8.	B	9.	B	10.	A	11.	B
12.	B	13.	B	14.	B	15.	B	16.	B

Chapter 5 – Loan Process
1. Approved   Everything contained within the file meets the guidelines for final approval

Conditional   Additional documentation will be needed to ensure final loan approval

Denied   Aspects of the file do not conform to the guidelines

2. Any individual who must complete their tasks in a timely, professional manner in order for you to accomplish your goal of closing the loan
3. The loan processor
4. By maintaining an organized flow process, using an adequate loan process follow-up and affinity service provider reminder-system.
5. By treating these providers in a respectful, friendly, and considerate manner to foster positive relationships, build rapport and create an overall good relationship.

6.	D	7	D	8	B	9	D	10	B
11	B	2	D	13	C	14	A	15	D

Chapter 6 – File Documentation

1. Department of Housing and Urban Development that is not a direct lender but rather maintains an ongoing program to monitor the quality of HUD originated loans.
2. Private Mortgage Insurance – a policy that protects the lenders who make loans to individuals without obtaining a full 20% down payment.
3. 5% of the loan amount paid at a rate of 1/12 of the overall premium monthly
4. Income before taxes
5. A compensating factor is any item that exists in the borrower's profile that falls outside of the standard or norm and may reflect favorably on the borrower from the perspective of the underwriter.

   A compensating factor may be used to overcome any item that exists in the borrower's profile that falls outside or exceeds standard guideline criteria.
6. All lenders require that a borrower have sufficient and adequate income to cover the repayment of the mortgage. The stability and probability of continuance must be established.
7. The probability that the borrower will repay their new mortgage in a timely manner
8. Verification of Mortgage
9. Combined Loan to Value
10. Generally, the higher the credit risks the higher percentage of funds the borrower must invest.
11. To ensure you are able to verify information, structure the loan package correctly, and request supporting information in an efficient manner.
12. Without proper documentation, the underwriter cannot make a valid decision on the loan package and will request additional items or stipulations prior to issuing an approval or conditional approval.
13. To assure the underwriter that you are aware of the lacking information and are working to obtain all necessary documentation.
14. To set a positive tone for the loan package

    To bring the compensating factors to the attention of the underwriter before they initially review the borrower profile

    To set the stage if something occurs later in the process that requires a positive decision or exception from the underwriter
15. This inclusion allows the underwriter to review the material and is a courtesy action that will smooth the underwriter's workload.
16. To allow the underwriter to request information required for loan decision, closing or secondary market sale and to provide clarification information regarding any file item that is unclear to the underwriter.

17.	C	18	B	19	29%	20	B	21	78%	22	A
23	D	24	A	25	D	26	A	27	D	28	B
29	A	30	B	31	A	32	B	33	A	34	B
35	C	36	C	37	C	38	A	39	B		

40 A system that relies on historical loan performance and statistical models to determine whether a loan will meet the requirements of a particular purchasing entity in the secondary market

41. Credit history   Collateral standards   Debt ratio
42. The speed with which the processes of the loan can be completed
43. A computer program set with specific standards and parameters compares the borrower's situation and no underwriter is required to review these specifics removing time considerations, backlog issues and human opinion.
44. To ensure that all applications, credit reports, debt and income information and other required documentation are correctly entered into the computer.
45. The package is submitted to underwriting using the traditional underwriting processes.

46.	B	47	D	48	C	49	B
50	B	51	C	52	A		

MORTGAGE LENDING APPENDIX D

Loan Processor Basic Training Lending Mathematics

DEBT-TO-INCOME RATIO EXCERCISES

To calculate a borrower's debt to income take the total monthly debt load and divide it by the total monthly income. For example:

A borrower who earns $2800.00 monthly and has installment debt of $750.00 monthly has a debt-to-income ratio of 26.78%.

$$\textbf{D} \qquad \textbf{I} \qquad \textbf{R}$$
$$750 \ / \ 2800 = 26.78\%$$

1. Income $6200
    Debt $1900
    Ratio   %

2. Income $3000
    Debt $1350
    Ratio   %

3. Income $3750
    Debt $ 970
    Ratio   %

4. Income $1600
    Debt $ 340
    Ratio   %

5. Income $2000
    Debt $ 420
    Ratio   %

6. Income $2480
    Debt $ 920
    Ratio   %

7. Income $4200
    Debt $1850
    Ratio   %

8. Income $4800
    Debt $2175
    Ratio   %

9. Income $5100
    Debt $1950
    Ratio   %

10. Income $5500
    Debt $1775
    Ratio   %

11. Income $5750
    Debt $1900
    Ratio   %

12. Income $3425
    Debt $1350
    Ratio   %

13. Income $4387
    Debt $1218
    Ratio   %

14. Income $2330
    Debt $ 961
    Ratio   %

Mortgage Lending – Home Mortgage Loan Processing

CALCULATING LOAN-TO-VALUE

When calculating loan to value, assuming the Value and the LTV Percentage are given the formula is Value multiplied by percentage.

Assume a house with a value (sales price) of $112,000 with a LTV of 95% would have a loan amount of $106,400.

Sales Price $112,000	x LTV Percentage x .95	= Loan Amount = $106,400

1. Sales Price $99,000
    LTV   85%

    Loan $

2. Sales Price $110,000
    LTV   90%

    Loan $

3. Sales Price $144,900
    LTV   95%

    Loan $

4. Sales Price $75,000
    LTV   80%

    Loan $

5. Sales Price $69,900
    LTV   70%

    Loan $

6. Sales Price $104,900
    LTV   75%

    Loan $

KENNEY

CALCULATING COMBINED LOAN TO VALUE

When a Combined Loan-to-Value is offered, you will calculate the secondary financing figure using the same formula above.

Sales Price	x CLTV Percentage	= Subordinate/Secondary Financing Loan Amount
$112,000	x .05	= $5600 maximum second mortgage

1. Sales Price $99,000

    LTV 85%   CLTV 95%

    Loan $ _____ $ _____

2. Sales Price $110,000

    LTV 90%   CLTV 95%

    Loan $ _____ $ _____

3. Sales Price $144,900

    LTV 90%   CLTV 95%

    Loan $ _____ $ _____

4. Sales Price $75,000

    LTV 80%   CLTV 90%

    Loan $ _____ $ _____

5. Sales Price $69,900

    LTV 70%   CLTV 80%

    Loan $ _____ $ _____

6. Sales Price $104,900

    LTV 75% CLTV 85%

    Loan $ _____ $ _____

Any funds toward the purchase price not included in LTV or CLTV will be required as cash invested on the part of the borrower. Funds for closing costs may be acquired through other means.

SELLER CONCESSION

When calculating seller concession toward borrower's non-recurring closing costs you will want to use the SALES PRICE of the property as your base number. The seller concession figure is negotiated in the sales agreement and can be a fixed dollar amount or it may be a percentage. For these exercises, assume the seller is willing to grant 6% of the sales price toward borrower's non-recurring closing costs.

Sales Price	x Concession Percentage	= Dollar Concession Amount
$112,000	x 6%	= $6720

1. Sales Price $99,000

2. Sales Price $110,000

3. Sales Price $144,900

4. Sales Price $75,000

5. Sales Price $69,900

6. Sales Price $104,900

7. Sales Price $49,500

8. Sales Price $219,900

9. Sales Price $53,350

10. Sales Price $189,000

SELLER CONCESSION

For additional exercise in calculating maximum seller concession, you can calculate using a maximum seller concession toward buyer's non-recurring closing costs of 3% of the sales price. (6% and 3% are the most commonly allowed maximum seller concessions under most underwriting guidelines.)

Sales Price	x Concession Percentage	= Dollar Concession Amount
$112,000	x 3%	= $3360

1. Sales Price $99,000

2. Sales Price $110,000

3. Sales Price $144,900

4. Sales Price $75,000

5. Sales Price $69,900

6. Sales Price $104,900

7. Sales Price $49,500

8. Sales Price $219,900

9. Sales Price $53,350

10. Sales Price $189,000

KENNEY

MAXIMUM HOUSING EXPENSE (PITI)

It is important to be able to calculate the maximum monthly housing expense (PITI – Principal, Interest, Taxes, and Insurance) your borrower could afford under any loan program approval. This allows you to set borrowers and Agents expectations as to the cost range of properties that the borrowers should be shopping.

Begin with the maximum DTI as per the approval level. Subtract the borrowers current DTI (excluding any housing expense from the ratio). The total is the percentage of income available to spend on PITI. This percentage should be multiplied by the borrower's total monthly income to achieve a maximum dollar amount that may be spent toward PITI.

The formula for calculating Maximum PITI payments is as follows:

Maximum DTI %	**– Current DTI %**	**= % Income Available for Housing Costs**
41%	- 22%	= 19%

Monthly Income	**X % of Income Available for PITI**	**= Maximum Mthly PITI**
$3200	X 19%	= $608 maximum PITI

For the following problems, assume a maximum DTI of 45%

1. Current DTI 29%
    Income $3750

2. Current DTI 18%
    Income $2100

3. Current DTI 22%
    Income $2880

4. Current DTI 31%
    Income $4195

5. Current DTI 24%
    Income $2655

6. Current DTI 12%
    Income $3875

7. Current DTI 19%
    Income $3150

8. Current DTI 26%
    Income $1775

9. Current DTI 14%
    Income $1980

10. Current DTI 36%
    Income $3650

LENDING MATH ANSWER KEY

DTI	RATIOS		SELLER CONCESSION 3%
1.	31%	1.	$2,970.00
2.	45%	2.	$3,300.00
3.	26%	3.	$4,347.00
4.	21%	4.	$2,250.00
5.	21%	5.	$2,097.00
6.	37%	6.	$3,147.00
7.	44%	7.	$1,485.00
8.	45%	8.	$6,597.00
9.	38%	9.	$1,600.50
10.	32%	10.	$5,670.00
11.	33%		
12.	39%		

MAXIMUM MONTHLY PITI PAYMENT

LTV			Ratio for PITI	$ Value for PITI
1.	$ 84,150	1.	12%	$ 450.00
2.	$ 99,000	2.	23%	$ 483.00
3.	$137,655	3.	19%	$ 547.20
4.	$ 60,000	4.	10%	$ 419.50
5.	$ 48,930	5.	17%	$ 451.35
6.	$ 78,675	6.	29%	$1123.75
		7.	22%	$ 693.00
CLTV		8.	15%	$ 266.25
1.	$ 9,900	9.	27%	$ 534.60
2.	$ 5,500	10.	5%	$ 182.50
3.	$ 7,245			
4.	$ 7,500			
5.	$ 6,990			
6.	$10,490			

SELLER CONCESSION 6%

1.	$ 5,940
2.	$ 6,600
3.	$ 8,694
4.	$ 4,500
5.	$ 4,194
6.	$ 6,294
7.	$ 2,970
8.	$13,194
9.	$ 3,201
10.	$11,340

www.ingramcontent.com/pod-product-compliance
Lightning Source LLC
Chambersburg PA
CBHW080239270326
41926CB00020B/4297